CHAPTER ONE
What Is Mammon?

Jesus was known for the direct way that He addressed issues in His teachings; He didn't throw words around under any circumstances. So when we study the gospels and the teachings of Jesus on money, we see that He was very clear about it. He actually used the word *mammon* at least four times in the gospels and, when He used it, He was not simply talking about money. He deliberately used the word *mammon* to show us what happens when we become *attached* to money. To go even further, mammon is the spirit that can become attached to money, as well as extend to every area of our lives if we are not careful. Its mission is to convince us that we don't need God and that we don't need to trust in Him to take care of us. Mammon is all about self-effort and doing things in our own ability. It is a spirit that tries to get us to trust in our money and our possessions, to think that these things are infallible and can't fail us. When we give in to the spirit of mammon, we set ourselves up for loss, pain, and, ultimately, destruction. In the book of Exodus, this spirit convinced the people that they didn't need God, and its strategy has not changed. It is an evil spirit that will deliberately lead us astray and abandon us. Even still, God will always extend His mercy and grace toward us when we need Him.

Mammon is not money; it is the spirit of deceitful riches that lies to us and tells us to trust our money instead of God. Jesus taught that if we are faithful in how we handle our finances, which means trusting God with all we have, we will be faithful with greater things in the kingdom of God. For the believer, mastering the financial realm is a responsibility that God does not take lightly. Among His many parables, Jesus talked about a steward who was unfaithful with his master's goods because he was influenced by the spirit of mammon (Luke 16:1-14). The original translation of *mammon* is "deceitful riches." What Jesus was teaching is that when money has the spirit of mammon on it, it becomes deceitful. It will betray you every time.

Always remember that money is neither good nor bad; it simply takes on the spirit of whoever has it in his or her possession. If a person is given over to a spirit of mammon, the money that comes into their hands will become deceitful. But if a person's life is controlled by the Spirit of God, their money will be under the influence of God and will be used for the right purposes. This is what allows God to promote a person to greater levels of financial prosperity. Mammon refers to the desire to pursue wealth as a primary goal in life, while the Bible says to seek God first, and everything else will be added (Matthew 6:33).

The spirit of mammon is the spirit of the devil. Jesus, Himself, was tempted by the devil in the wilderness and He passed the test with flying colors. Matthew 4:8, 9 says, *"Again, the devil taketh him up into an exceeding high mountain, and sheweth him all the kingdoms of the world, and the glory of them; And saith unto him, All these things will I give thee, if thou wilt fall down and worship me."* Mammon tried to seduce Jesus with the very thing He came to restore back to mankind—authority in the earth realm. If he tried to get Jesus to bow to mammon, he will most definitely attempt to get us to do the same. We have to resist Him by declaring the Word of God and standing strong in our reliance on God as our source.

DON'T MAKE MAMMON YOUR GOD

Just like he tempted Jesus in the wilderness, Satan wants to get us to bow our knee to him in worship. When we allow mammon to control our lives and decisions, that is exactly what we are doing. Mammon becomes our god when we give in to Satan's suggestions to trust in our money and material possessions.

The Word of God is our answer when the spirit of mammon comes knocking at our door. When fear, anxiety, and worry over financial concerns show up, you can quickly identify it as an attack from mammon and turn to the Scriptures to shut it down. Philippians 4:6 says, *"Be careful for nothing; but in every thing by prayer and supplication with thanksgiving let your requests be made known unto God."* We are told to be anxious for nothing because being anxious is a sign that we worship mammon. Those who trust in God are not anxious about their financial situation; they rest in the finished works of Jesus. We have to make a quality decision to stop being perpetually uneasy, anxious, and worried about how bills are going to be paid and how our needs are going to be met. These things are *God's* responsibility, not ours. Our job is to seek His way of doing things, *first,* and then all things will be added to our lives (Matthew 6:33, 34).

As believers, we are to live in the present instead of projecting our worries and fears into the future. When we choose to live day by day, trusting Him in every moment for all of our needs and desires, financial or otherwise, the Holy Spirit will give us the grace we need to get to the next point. We don't have to fear the future. We rely on God and His ability, not our own. This type of unwavering trust in God dismantles the spirit of mammon and strips it of its power in our lives.

Study Questions

1. True or False: Jesus frequently taught about money.

2. True or False: The influence of mammon can extend beyond the financial realm of your life.

3. What is mammon's mission? _____

4. Mammon is all about _____.

5. Mammon is not money, it is the spirit of _____ riches.

6. If we are faithful with how we handle our finances, we will be faithful with _____.

7. True or False: Money is neither good nor bad.

8. What did mammon try to seduce Jesus with? _____

9. Mammon becomes our god when we _____.

10. As believers, how are we to live? _____

SCRIPTURE REFERENCES

Luke 16:1-14

Matthew 6:33

Matthew 4:8, 9

Philippians 4:6

Matthew 6:24-34

Luke 19:2-24

CHAPTER TWO
Mammon: The Spirit of Satan

When studying the Word of God, it is so important to pay attention to context and not try to apply any one Scripture to any and all situations. To do so is to miss so much of what God is trying to say and its true meaning. Over time, we can accumulate the wrong information and reach incorrect assumptions because we *wrongly* divide the Word, which leads to wrong-believing and, inevitably, wrong-living. It is dangerous to take the Scriptures about money and misapply them. When Jesus talked about money, His main goal was to drive the point home about how critical it is to trust God. The condition of a person's heart is often revealed by how they handle money because wealth always seems to magnify the character traits that are already present in a person's life. Money is just a tool, but the spirit of mammon tries to use it to undermine our trust in God and redirect it into material possessions. We must remain vigilant not to allow the spirit of mammon, which is the spirit of Satan, to infiltrate our hearts.

The spirit of mammon is a demonic spirit that is designed to steal, kill, and destroy. It starts by getting us to turn our focus away from God and onto ourselves, our ability, and our possessions. Jesus taught about money management and how to successfully navigate the financial realm in many of His teachings. A study of the Scriptures reveals that

His primary message was about trusting God for all of our needs and refusing to allow our trust to be in our possessions.

Luke 16 reveals the core of Jesus' teaching on money:

He that is faithful in that which is least is faithful also in much: and he that is unjust in the least is unjust also in much. If therefore ye have not been faithful in the unrighteous mammon, who will commit to your trust the true riches? And if ye have not been faithful in that which is another man's, who shall give you that which is your own? No servant can serve two masters: for either he will hate the one, and love the other; or else he will hold to the one, and despise the other. Ye cannot serve God and mammon. And the Pharisees also, who were covetous, heard all these things: and they derided him (Luke 16:10-15).

Jesus' message was this: our relationship with the financial realm is of utmost importance to God. Money is the least in the kingdom of God, and if we are faithful with what God considers the least, it demonstrates that we will also be faithful with much more. But if we fail to show ourselves faithful with money, how can God entrust us with the deeper and bigger things of His kingdom? The truth is that we cannot serve God *and* serve the god of mammon; we must choose to whom we will serve and submit.

Everything about our lives is based on how we are influenced by money. Think about it: we make decisions based on how much money we have, it often controls our emotions, and we invest our time and lives into obtaining more of it. Money tends to control so much of what we do and how we move through this life that we often don't realize the amount of concern we exert when it comes to money. God is a spirit, but so is mammon. It is the spirit behind a wrong relationship with money. We must choose which spirit will be our master. Mammon involves covetousness, which is connected to greed; and greed causes a person to do everything they can to get material possessions and hold on to them. When you are controlled by this spirit, you will abandon your values just to get more money. It is a wicked influence in a person's life.

Mammon is in direct opposition to the will of God. It was the spirit that influenced Peter to rebuke Jesus when He said He had to go to the cross and die (Matthew 16:22, 23). Although what Peter said sounded noble, and like it was coming from a place of care and concern, Satan was motivating him, and Jesus rebuked Peter for trying to stand in the way of God's plans. That's just what you have to do when the spirit of mammon tries to hinder the will of God for your life. As Christians, we must know the Word of God well enough to discern when we are being influenced by the spirit of mammon. Jesus recognized the spirit of mammon speaking through Peter, as well as the Pharisees whom He rebuked many times for their covetousness and greed. Jesus can see into our hearts. He knows when we are operating in a spirit that is in opposition to His will and plan for our lives.

First John 2:15-17 instructs us not to love the world or the things of this world system because when we love the things of the world, the love of the Father is not in us. All that is in this world system, the lust of the eyes, the lust of the flesh, and the pride of life, ultimately lead to destruction. These things will all pass away, but he who does the will of God will have everlasting life. The spirit of mammon controls the world system and everything in it; it will eventually pass away, as well. God, His Word, and His kingdom will never pass away, which is why we want to align ourselves with the will of God and turn away from the spirit of mammon.

THE LIES OF MAMMON

Satan is the father of lies and, since the spirit of mammon is one and the same with the enemy, it will constantly lie to us and tell us that it is more trustworthy than God. The truth is that we can *always* trust God in any situation and for anything we will ever need. He will never fail us or forsake us. There is no person or spirit outside of God that we can rely on to provide for us or care for us. We certainly cannot believe the lie that mammon tells us, that it can take care of us better than God can. Neither can we trust in ourselves, which is also a lie of mammon.

In the book of Luke, we see the provision of Jesus in the lives of His disciples. It says, *"And he said unto them, When I sent you without purse, and scrip, and shoes, lacked ye any thing? And they said, Nothing. Then said he unto them, But now, he that hath a purse, let him take it, and likewise his scrip: and he that hath no sword, let him sell his garment, and buy one"* (Luke 22:35, 36). Jesus asked this question of His disciples to test them and get them to realize in whom they could put their trust—Him. Once they realized they lacked nothing because God was taking care of them on their journey, Jesus told them to retrieve their earthly possessions. We can read this Scripture as if Jesus is asking us the same question. When you really think about your life, you can see God's hand of provision in place no matter your situation or circumstance. Like He did for the disciples, Jesus has provided for you. For this reason, you can rely on Him as your only source.

The story of the rich young ruler shows us how the spirit of mammon will lie to a person to get him or her to trust in possessions more than God:

> And when he was gone forth into the way, there came one running, and kneeled to him, and asked him, Good Master, what shall I do that I may inherit eternal life? And Jesus said unto him, Why callest thou me good? there is none good but one, that is, God. Thou knowest the commandments, Do not commit adultery, Do not steal, Do not bear false witness, Defraud not, Honour thy father and mother. And he answered and said unto him, Master,

all these have I observed from my youth. Then Jesus beholding him loved him, and said unto him, One thing thou lackest: go thy way, sell whatsoever thou hast, and give to the poor, and thou shalt have treasure in heaven: and come, take up the cross, and follow me. And he was sad at that saying, and went away grieved: for he had great possessions. And Jesus looked round about, and saith unto his disciples, How hardly shall they that have riches enter into the kingdom of God! And the disciples were astonished at his words. But Jesus answereth again, and saith unto them, Children, how hard is it for them that trust in riches to enter into the kingdom of God! (Mark 10:17-24).

Jesus tested this young ruler's character by telling him to give away his money. This was the same test He had shared with the disciples in Luke 16. The young man's reaction revealed what he trusted more—his possessions. This rich young ruler was controlled by the spirit of mammon and, as a result, he missed out on an opportunity to be a part of Jesus' dynamic ministry. The man didn't have riches—his riches had him. He saw giving as a loss instead of a gain and it held him back from experiencing promotion. That's what happens when we give ourselves over to mammon; it stops us from laying hold of the promises of God for our lives.

Jesus also told the parable of the man traveling to a far country who gave his servants talents according to their abilities. When he returned, he learned that two of them multiplied their talents, but the third one had buried his in the ground and done nothing with it (Matthew 25:14-30). The man who received only one talent and kept it hidden displayed covetousness. He admitted he was afraid, which shows that he was under mammon's influence. Anytime fear is present as it relates to stewardship and finances, mammon is in full operation. On the other hand, when we trust God with everything He gives us, we will obey His leading with our resources and experience increase.

Nothing about the spirit of mammon is for our good. In fact, mammon will lead us far away from the Spirit of God, and then abandon us. Judas Iscariot is an example of someone who allowed the spirit of mammon to get in his heart. It led him to his demise after using him to betray Jesus. Ananias and his wife, Sapphira, also allowed the spirit of mammon to overtake them and then lied to Peter about the money they received from a piece of property they sold. Judas, Ananias, and Sapphira met their deaths as a result of the spirit of mammon directing their decisions. It is a spirit that will leave us buried in a grave and following it will always leave us in a ditch. The *love* of money is the root of all evil and, when we allow it to take possession of our hearts, we *will* go astray; but when we make God our choice and our source, money will become our slave and it has to obey us.

There is nothing wrong with having money; in fact, it is God's will that we have possessions and money, but only if they are under His influence. The Bible promises that wealth and riches will be in the house of those who have been declared righteous (Psalm 112:3). Proverbs 10:22 also says that the blessing of the Lord makes us rich, and God adds no sorrow to our lives when the blessing is operating. We are not to trust in riches, but understand that God gives us all things richly to enjoy and that it is His will that we prosper and enjoy abundant life.

Jesus warned against greed in the parable of the rich man who had plenty of material wealth and decided to store it up for himself. The problem was that all of his possessions had no eternal value. When it comes to matters of eternity and the soul, one's riches are irrelevant. God wants us to store up treasures in heaven by developing a thriving relationship with Him and doing His will, versus striving to acquire more money at the expense of our souls (Luke 12:13-21). He warns against greed but does not want us to live in poverty. The issue is making sure that we don't have a wrong relationship with the material realm.

Religion tells us that we are materialistic if we believe God for money, but materialism does not mean having material things; materialism is an attempt to use materials to replace God. This is a form of idolatry that is driven by the spirit of mammon. Religion also tells us that we should use moderation when it comes to the material realm, yet heaven is described as lavish and extravagant in the Word of God. Philippians says, *"Rejoice in the Lord always: and again I say, Rejoice. Let your moderation be known unto all men. The Lord is at hand"* (Philippians 4:4, 5). The dictionary defines *moderation* as the avoidance of extremes or excesses; however, the Greek word here that was translated "moderation" means unselfishness, consideration, and forbearance. Context is everything and when the word *moderation* is used in context, we see that God is talking about having an unselfish attitude. He is not saying it is wrong to have material possessions.

If we are going to truly prosper in the things of God, we have to understand God's heart behind every matter He addresses in His Word. As we grow in our relationship with Him and understand His heart, we will see that trusting Him for every area of our lives is the way to avoid succumbing to the spirit of mammon. By renewing our minds with a true understanding of God's Word, we can experience the increase and promotion He has prepared for us and avoid the traps and lies of the spirit of mammon. When we master the money issue, we can move on to greater things in the kingdom of God!

Study Questions

1. What happens when we take Scripture out of context? _____
   _____

2. What was Jesus' main point when He talked about money?
   _____

3. How is the condition of a person's heart often revealed?
   _____

4. Money is just a _____.

5. The spirit of mammon is designed to _____,
   _____, and _____.

6. Money is the _____ in the kingdom of God.

7. We cannot serve God and _____.

8. True or False: There is nothing wrong with having money.

9. True or False: Riches are irrelevant when it comes to the eternal condition of your soul.

10. What is materialism? _____
    _____

SCRIPTURE REFERENCES

Luke 16:10-15

Matthew 16:22, 23

1 John 2:15-17

Luke 22:35, 36

Mark 10:17-24

Matthew 25:14-30

Psalm 112:3

Proverbs 10:22

Luke 12:13-21

Philippians 4:4-6

Matthew 6:33

Matthew 4:8, 9

Luke 19:2-24

Matthew 6:24-34

CHAPTER THREE
Unmasking the Spirit of Mammon

One of the most revealing ways we can determine how much we trust God is found in how we handle our finances. Throughout the Scriptures, we see the wisdom of God as it relates to money. Unfortunately, many in the body of Christ don't want to acknowledge the importance of money and how God wants us to handle it. Money is simply a tool, and it does not carry a spirit on it, in and of itself, until we take possession of it. If *we* are under the influence of mammon, which is an evil spirit in direct contradiction to God, that spirit will influence how we handle the money we have. If *we* are directed by the Spirit of God, *His* Spirit will influence our management of money. Because the Spirit of God and the spirit of mammon are in direct opposition to each other, *we* are the ones who will have to choose which one we will allow to operate in our lives. Mammon hides behind a mask of lies and pretends it can do what only God can do. It wants to set itself up as our source, but we have to fight against its operation. If we are to remove this mask and see the truth clearly, we must deliberately choose to serve God and not mammon.

It is so vital to understand that there is nothing wrong with prosperity, as long as it does not turn our hearts from God. Jesus taught about the financial realm frequently in His ministry so it would serve us well to pay attention to what He had to say. Luke 16 gives us clear insight into the fundamentals of money stewardship in the life of a believer:

> He that is faithful in that which is least is faithful also in much: and he that is unjust in the least is unjust also in much. If therefore ye have not been faithful in the unrighteous mammon, who will commit to your trust the true riches? And if ye have not been faithful in that which is another man's, who shall give you that which is your own? No servant can serve two masters: for either he will hate the one, and love the other; or else he will hold to the one, and despise the other. Ye cannot serve God and mammon (Luke 16:10-13).

What Jesus was teaching here was that how we handle ourselves where money is concerned determines how we handle ourselves in other areas of our lives. It also determines whether we can handle greater responsibilities in the kingdom of God. When we use faith in our finances, this is the least use of our faith in the kingdom of God. It is okay to have possessions, as long as what we have is under the right management. If they are, they will be a blessing. If they are not, they will be hoarded instead of being used to help others. We simply have to get this area of money together if we are going to see more of what God wants to do in our lives.

First John 2:15, 16 gives us some instruction on how to avoid becoming ensnared by the spirit of mammon: "*Love not the world, neither the things that are in the world. If any man love the world, the love of the Father is not in him. For all that is in the world, the lust of the flesh, and the lust of the eyes, and the pride of life, is not of the Father, but is of the world.*" If we love the world, then, by default, we have chosen *not* to love God; there is no middle ground. Mammon is the spirit governing this world's system which is comprised of the lust of the flesh, the lust of the eyes, and the pride of life. The pride of life is a life that does not submit itself to the Word of God, the lust of the eyes is a strong appetite to get everything we see, and the lust of the flesh is a desire for everything that nourishes self-centeredness. When we allow these things to have place in our lives, we open the door to mammon, which will ultimately destroy us.

The spirit of mammon does not work alone, but in conjunction with the spirits of pride, greed, and poverty. Pride refuses to acknowledge God for His blessings and it refuses to obey what God says to do. Pride actually blocks the flow of God's grace (James 4:6). It is the spirit of mammon that caused Lucifer to lose his position in heaven and fall. It is a liar and it causes us to turn away from the spirit of God.

Greed is the spirit of the world. It causes us to hold on to everything we have and seek even more. Stinginess is related to greed, and it will always leave us lacking. When God speaks to us and tells us to give, it is always for our benefit, not His (Psalm 50:9-15). Therefore, whatever He says to sow or give, when we obey His instructions, we are going to win. We must not allow the spirit of mammon to steal the blessings of being a cheerful giver. When God says give, move quickly with an obedient heart that is committed to giving God first place.

Finally, the spirit of poverty is connected to the spirit of mammon and causes us to be ashamed of God's blessings in our lives. It seduces us so that we will not want to claim what He gives us. The spirit of poverty is particularly dangerous because it contradicts the Word and His plan for people to experience financial prosperity. God is responsible for the good things that happen to us, including our material blessings, and we should openly declare His goodness to us (Psalm 118:23). Poverty fights against the knowledge that God desires to increase us and *does* increase us! It wants to deny us abundant grace and all sufficiency in all things. It all boils down to an issue of who we trust. When we put our faith in money, we are headed for trouble (Proverbs 11:28).

BE HONEST WITH GOD

The truth is that we cannot lie to God about our intentions when it comes to wealth; He knows our hearts. Ananias and his wife, Sapphira, tried lying to the Holy Spirit and it cost them their lives (Acts 5:1-11). These two had sold a possession and laid most of the proceeds at the apostles' feet, but held on to some of the profit. Peter asked Ananias why Satan had filled his heart to lie to the Holy Spirit and, when Ananias heard these words, he fell down dead. When Sapphira arrived later, Peter questioned her about the price, and she also lied. She also fell down dead after Peter asked her why she had lied to the Holy Spirit. Ananias and Sapphira tried to scam the people and this is an example of the spirit of mammon at work. Mammon influenced them to lie about the money. Nothing escapes God, not even our hearts' deepest motives. We can't be afraid to give freely and hold nothing back from God (Luke 6:38).

A powerful example of someone who gave freely to bless God is Mary Magdalene. She took a pound of costly spikenard perfume, anointed Jesus' feet with it, and wiped them with her hair. Mary was under the influence of the Spirit of God, but Judas, who would later betray Jesus, rebuked her for wasting such a costly ointment. He said the money from the sale of the perfume could be used to give to the poor, even though he was actually stealing from the treasury (John 12:3-6). Judas' true character and nature were demonstrated in these moments of Mary's generosity. He only cared about money because he was driven by the spirit of mammon. In addition, Judas had a problem with Jesus receiving a gesture of prosperity from Mary. We must take note of anyone around us who has a problem with how God is blessing us and beware of them.

Whenever Jesus talked about money, He was really talking about trust. Trust is really what this whole money issue is about. He also wants us to maximize the money that we do have. The parable of the talents is a great example of this:

> For the kingdom of heaven is as a man travelling into a far country, who called his own servants, and delivered unto them his goods. And unto one he gave five talents, to another two, and to another one; to every man according to his several ability; and straightway took his journey. Then he that had received the five talents went and traded with the same, and made them other five talents. And likewise he that had received two, he also gained other two. But he that had received one went and digged in the earth, and hid his lord's money. After a long time the lord of those servants cometh, and reckoneth with them. And so he that had received five talents came and brought other five talents, saying, Lord, thou deliveredst unto me five talents: behold, I have gained beside them five talents more. His lord said unto him, Well done, thou good and faithful servant: thou hast been faithful over a few things, I will make thee ruler over many things: enter thou into the joy of thy lord. He also that had received two talents came and said, Lord, thou deliveredst unto me two talents: behold, I have gained two other talents beside them. His lord said unto him, Well done, good and faithful servant; thou hast been faithful over a few things, I will make thee ruler over many things: enter thou into the joy of thy lord. Then he which had received the one talent came and said, Lord, I knew thee that thou art an hard man, reaping where thou hast

not sown, and gathering where thou hast not strawed: And I was afraid, and went and hid thy talent in the earth: lo, there thou hast that is thine. His lord answered and said unto him, Thou wicked and slothful servant, thou knewest that I reap where I sowed not, and gather where I have not strawed: Thou oughtest therefore to have put my money to the exchangers, and then at my coming I should have received mine own with usury. Take therefore the talent from him, and give it unto him which hath ten talents. For unto every one that hath shall be given, and he shall have abundance: but from him that hath not shall be taken away even that which he hath (Matthew 25:14-29).

This parable lets us know how God feels about our money management. Jesus was pleased with the first two men who multiplied their money, calling them good and faithful, but He was displeased with the third man who hid his talent in the ground out of greed. God wants us to make the most of the blessings He gives us and not hoard our resources. When we steward God's things with wisdom and integrity, our money multiplies and we have even more to present to God when He asks it of us.

The spirit of mammon has no place in the life of a believer and it can be overcome by making a quality decision to trust God and keep money in its proper place in our lives. It is given to us to be stewarded, not hoarded. Becoming faithful with your finances pleases God and keeps the spirit of mammon from infiltrating. Trust God with everything you have and watch Him open the door to blessings you cannot even comprehend!

Study Questions

1. What does the parable of the unfaithful steward demonstrate to us? _____

2. What is mammon? _____

3. What does mammon cause us to do? _____

4. True or False: Those who are faithful with money will be faithful with greater things.

5. Tue or False: Money is the biggest component in the kingdom of God.

6. How do you know mammon is influencing you? _____

7. What are the four questions we must ask ourselves to determine if mammon is influencing us? _____
_____
_____
_____

8. If you are born again, your only source is _____.

9. How can you stay focused on God's ability? _____

SCRIPTURE REFERENCES

Luke 16:10-13

1 John 2:15, 16

James 4:6

Psalm 50:9-15

Psalm 118:23

Proverbs 11:28

Acts 5:1-11

Luke 6:38

John 12:3-6

Matthew 25:14-29

Mark 12:41-44

Matthew 6:21

Isaiah 14:12-15

Nehemiah 8:10

CHAPTER FOUR
Three Spirits of Mammon

The devil always comes to us with a multi-pronged attack; it is rare that a particular spirit is being released against us by itself. In the case of the spirit of mammon, we must examine its influence in the spiritual realm. Although we cannot see this realm with our physical eyes, it is as real as the natural world in which we live. The spirit of mammon attaches itself to money and, if we are not careful, we can fall under its subtle influence. Its goal is to exert demonic influence in the area of our finances. It tries to trick us into trusting money more than we trust God by slightly twisting the truth of the Word just enough to confuse us. We are susceptible to this type of trickery if we do not know the Word of God well enough to see through mammon's lies. Demonic influence always takes advantage of an ignorant Christian, which is why it is so important for us to acquire biblical knowledge and stand strong against attacks in this area.

Mammon attaches itself to money, and to our attitudes. It may seem strange to us to talk about spirits, but the spiritual world is real. We are spiritual beings possessing souls and living in physical bodies. God is also a spirit (John 4:24), and all physical things are the result of spiritual things. We must understand the influences that come from the spiritual realm in order to understand the Word of God.

Jesus said that he who is faithful with little is also faithful in much, and he who is unjust in the least is also unjust in much (Luke 16:10-13). He taught that if we are not faithful with money, how can we be entrusted with true riches? We cannot serve God and mammon. Jesus was explaining that the least use of our faith in the kingdom of God is in the area of money. The "much" refers to all the things that have been made available to us by God's grace—healing, deliverance, the gifts of the Spirit, and more. How we manage the financial realm is what qualifies us to manage the greater things of the spiritual realm.

Faith and trust go hand in hand, and our willingness to give is an indication of our level of trust. In fact, God will give us opportunities to demonstrate that we trust Him and then observe us to see what we do. A great example of this is the story of the widow who cast her mites into the treasury. Although there were others there who were giving large amounts of money, Jesus considered her the biggest giver of them all because she gave *all* she had (Mark 12:41-44). The question we must always answer for ourselves is whether the Spirit of God or the spirit of mammon is motivating us concerning finances. When we to want to hold on to what we have with a stingy heart, we can be sure that the spirit of mammon is controlling us.

As stated earlier, the spirit of mammon extends farther than money; it wants to exert an evil influence in every area of our lives, while the Spirit of God wants to exert a godly influence. We can see this godly influence in the life of Simon Peter when Jesus asked him who people said He was in Matthew 16:13-18. Peter received direct revelation from the Father about the identity of Jesus as the Son of the living God, but right after this exchange, we see mammon's influence on Peter's soul when he rebuked Jesus:

From that time forth began Jesus to shew unto his disciples, how that he must go unto Jerusalem, and suffer many things of the elders and chief priests and scribes, and be killed, and be raised again the third day. Then Peter took him, and began to rebuke him, saying, Be it far from thee, Lord: this shall not be unto thee. But he turned, and said unto Peter, Get thee behind me, Satan: thou art an offence unto me: for thou savourest not the things that be of God, but those that be of men (Matthew 16:21-23).

When Peter verbally opposed what Jesus revealed, his words sounded good, and even appeared to reflect concern and love for Jesus. However, what Peter said opposed the will of God for Jesus' life. It was the spirit of mammon in operation trying to stop the plan of salvation from coming to pass. In our lives, we will also hear things that sound godly, but they will not line up with the Scriptures. There is no way of knowing truth from lies until we get into the Word of God and truly discover Him for ourselves (Psalm 46:10).

MAMMON'S INFLUENCE OVER MONEY

We do not wrestle against flesh and blood but against spiritual wickedness in high places (Ephesians 6:12). The spirit of mammon is one of these demonic forces. The predominant weapon that demons use against us is the weapon of suggestion. We fight against their influence by standing on what we know from God's Word and renewing our minds with the truth that we discover. We engage in spiritual warfare by maintaining the victory that Jesus died for us to obtain. The devil has no defense against a Christian who is rooted and grounded in the truth of the Word and knows what has been made available to him or her through the finished works of Jesus. Satan is defeated when we continue to stand on the Word just the way Jesus did when He was tempted in the wilderness (Matthew 4:1-11; Luke 4:1-13). We must remember who we are in Christ because the kingdom of darkness knows when we are secure in our identity in Jesus.

The way mammon exerts its influence over our money is by getting us to give our hearts over to the love of money. Contrary to what religion teaches, money is not the root of all evil—the *love* of money is the problem. First Timothy 6:10 says that those who allow their hearts to be taken with the *love* of money turn away from the faith and open themselves up to a variety of problems in life. Love is a relational word. The love of money actually describes a wrong relationship with the material realm. Mammon promotes this type of relationship and draws us away from God. If we truly want to locate where our hearts are and what we really love, we must examine our relationship with money and make adjustments if necessary. Looking at how we spend our time and money will tell the story. Sometimes we will discover that our hearts are actually *not* with God. If this is the case, we simply need to repent and recommit ourselves to making God our source.

THE THREE SPIRITS OF MAMMON

Demonic spirits often cluster together so that they can wreak the most havoc in people's lives. The spirit of mammon has three "cousins" that seek to steal, kill, and destroy. The first is pride. Pride is basically a refusal to acknowledge God and His Word as the final authority; it also refuses to acknowledge God as the source of the blessings we receive in life. Pride is all about self-effort and making things happen on our own. It is a spirit that is in direct opposition to the Word of God. Pride causes us to turn away from God and seek our own self-satisfaction, thereby making us into our own god. It is a lie, so when we have a prideful life, we live a lie. Pride makes us compare ourselves to others and overlook what God is doing in our lives. It is destructive and always leads to a fall.

The second spirit that is attached to the spirit of mammon is the spirit of greed. Keep in mind that we do not need money to be greedy. It is okay to have possessions, as long as they do not have us. God says to give and bless others, but greed causes us to hold on to everything we have and seek even more. When a spirit of greed overtakes a person's life, they can never have enough and are never satisfied with what they do have.

Finally, the spirit of poverty works in conjunction with the spirit of mammon to cause us to be ashamed of God's blessings. It puts us in a state of constant want. God is able to make all grace abound toward us, so that we always have all that we need in every situation and circumstance we face (2 Corinthians 9:8). The spirit of poverty does not want this to happen in our lives, but instead wants us to cower under lack and hide what God is doing for us.

Overcoming the spirit of mammon in a world that is controlled by it is no easy feat in our own ability. However, Jesus has already overcome the world and everything that is in it. When we are in Christ and rely on the grace of God to empower us to overcome the devil in our everyday lives, we will walk in victory over the spirit of mammon. Practicing the presence of God and allowing Him to be our priority, especially when it comes to money matters, keeps Satan under our feet. Rebel against the spirit of mammon and the trio of pride, greed, and poverty by acknowledging God in all your ways and purposing in your heart to live a giving lifestyle. This way you prove your faithfulness in the "least" in the kingdom of God, which is "money."

Study Questions

1. What is mammon's goal? _____

2. When are we most susceptible to mammon's influence? _____
   _____

3. Mammon attaches itself to our _____
   and _____.

4. All physical things are the result of _____.

5. What is the biggest indicator of our trust in God? _____
   _____

6. Why did Jesus consider the woman who gave two mites the biggest giver? _____

7. What are the three spirits attached to mammon? _____
   _____

8. What does the spirit of poverty cause us to do? _____
   _____

9. What is spiritual warfare? _____
   _____

10. How can you rebel against the spirit of mammon? _____
    _____

SCRIPTURE REFERENCES

John 4:24

Luke 16:10-13

Mark 12:41-44

Matthew 16:13-18, 21-23

Psalm 46:10

Ephesians 6:12

Matthew 4:1-11

Luke 4:1-13

1 Timothy 6:10

2 Corinthians 9:8

CHAPTER FIVE
Mammon's Agenda

If there is one thing that truly tests a person's character, it is money and how they handle it. We can learn so much about ourselves and others by how we handle finances. Thankfully, the Bible is the ultimate "money guide," teaching us how to be faithful in financial affairs so that we can walk in the weightier matters of God's kingdom. The way Jesus taught on money is quite different from the religious message we often hear that says money management is not an indicator of character. However, money is very important. This is why Jesus spent so much time preaching about it. God wants us to put our trust in Him alone, not only with our finances but with every other area of our lives. When we don't trust God with our money, the spirit of mammon can attach itself to our resources. This spirit's influence is so prevalent in the world today that many people don't even realize they are actually worshipping money. That's mammon's agenda: to get us to bow down to money and abandon our trust in God. This spirit is in direct opposition to everything godly and it has a variety of ways to subtly infiltrate our lives. We must be vigilant to guard against the spirit of mammon and put God first in our finances.

The spirit of mammon has been around a long time. In fact, it has been lurking on the earth since Adam and Eve took up residence in the garden of Eden. This spirit has one agenda: to get you to abandon God as your source and trust in your money, your ability, your intellect, and your way of doing things, apart from God. Mammon is sneaky and hides behind money with the sole purpose of opposing God's will.

Jesus taught that money is actually the least in the kingdom of God, and when you are faithful with the least (money), God can entrust you with more. Luke 16:10-14 says:

> He that is faithful in that which is least is faithful also in much: and he that is unjust in the least is unjust also in much. If therefore ye have not been faithful in the unrighteous mammon, who will commit to your trust the true riches? And if ye have not been faithful in that which is another man's, who shall give you that which is your own? No servant can serve two masters: for either he will hate the one, and love the other; or else he will hold to the one, and despise the other. Ye cannot serve God and mammon. And the Pharisees also, who were covetous, heard all these things: and they derided him.

When interpreting Scriptures, it is important not to lift things out of context. Doing so can lead to bad doctrine. In this passage, Jesus makes a distinction between money and mammon. He calls money the least, then says you can't serve God and mammon at the same time. While the Aramaic translation of "mammon" means money or riches, it comes from the concept of the Syrian god of riches. When Jesus used the word mammon here, He was referring to a false god and the spirit behind that false god with whom the Syrians were familiar.

Mammon is rooted in Babylonian history. It means "sown in confusion." Babylon is known for the tower of Babel, a situation in which the people believed they did not need God to do what they were trying to do. They thought their work was enough to get them into heaven, which is what the spirit of mammon wants us to believe. It is a spirit that is determined to draw us away from God and get us immersed in self-effort.

Mammon is a spirit, an attitude, and an influence that tells us that if we have money, we do not need God. This is the spirit of Satan, himself. The dictionary definition of mammon is the god of riches and greed. When this spirit is in operation in your finances, you will start to trust in your money, feel that you will do almost anything to get more money, and never be satisfied with the money you do have. You will compromise your values and morals for it and abandon your faith in God as your source.

Satan tried to get Jesus to bow to the spirit of mammon when he tempted Him in the wilderness. Matthew 4:8-10 says, *"Again, the devil taketh him up into an exceeding high mountain, and sheweth him all the kingdoms of the world, and the glory of them; And saith unto him, All these things will I give thee, if thou wilt fall down and worship me. Then saith Jesus unto him, Get thee hence, Satan: for it is written, Thou shalt worship the Lord thy God, and him only shalt thou serve."* Jesus already had an answer for Satan's insidious attempt to tempt Him with the very things Jesus came to restore back to mankind. Like Jesus, we also have to make a decision to worship God, only, and refuse to bow to the spirit of mammon. Although Jesus was God, He was also man. He was just as susceptible to yielding to Satan as we are had He not made a choice. Jesus placed His relationship with the Father above everything and refused to allow the spirit of mammon to take Him off course.

GOD'S PRESENCE ELIMINATES MAMMON'S INFLUENCE

The spirit of mammon cannot thrive in the presence of God, for obvious reasons. Nothing that is anti-God can survive when it comes in contact with Jesus. There are examples of this throughout the Bible, but one particular example that deals with the spirit of mammon bowing to God was when Jesus encountered Zacchaeus:

> And Jesus entered and passed through Jericho. And, behold, there was a man named Zacchaeus, which was the chief among the publicans, and he was rich. And he sought to see Jesus who he was; and could not for the press, because he was little of stature. And he ran before, and climbed up into a sycomore tree to see him: for he was to pass that way. And when Jesus came to the place, he looked up, and saw him, and said unto him, Zacchaeus, make haste, and come down; for to day I must abide at thy house. And he made haste, and came down, and received him joyfully. And when they saw it, they all murmured, saying, That he was gone to be guest with a man that is a sinner. And Zacchaeus stood, and said unto the Lord: Behold, Lord, the half of my goods I give to the poor; and if I have taken any thing from any man by false accusation, I restore him fourfold. And Jesus said unto him, This day is salvation come to this house, forsomuch as he also is a son of Abraham (Luke 19:1-9).

What makes this story so powerful is that Zacchaeus was a publican. Publicans were known to be driven by the spirit of mammon in their dealings with people. Zacchaeus was considered a sinner, someone with whom the religious leaders of the day definitely would not associate. He had climbed a tree just to see Jesus pass through and, when He did, Jesus called him out, telling Zacchaeus that He would come to his house. It was during that encounter in Zacchaeus' home that Zacchaeus was so impacted by Jesus his entire perspective changed. He went from being a man of greed to a man who said he would give half his goods to the poor and restore what he had taken from people through false accusation.

The spirit of mammon fled during one encounter with God. Jesus didn't say anything about money, but His presence, alone, was enough to cause Zacchaeus to repent, disconnect from the spirit of mammon, and completely embrace a giving lifestyle. His decision to become a giver opened the door for salvation to come to his household and for good things to happen there that previously could not happen. He essentially became a partaker of the covenant of Abraham.

In Jesus' parable of the nobleman who went into a far country, what qualified the first two servants for more authority was their faithfulness in the least, which was money (Luke 19:12-26). This parable made the same point as the previous one about a rich man who wanted to build bigger barns to store all his goods (Luke 12:16-21). Faithfulness in the financial arena is the key to promotion in the kingdom of God because it truly is the least.

SIX SIGNS THAT MAMMON IS CONTROLLING YOUR LIFE

There are some very specific signs you can look for to determine if the spirit of mammon is in operation in your life. Let's take a look at them:

1. You feel anxiety over unmet needs.

Whenever you feel anxiety over unmet needs, it is an indicator that mammon is present. God is our provider; but we buy into mammon's philosophy when we live under financial fantasies where greed rules. We are to trust God entirely for all of our needs to be met on every level. When you are soaking in the presence of God, your trust in Him will skyrocket and the anxiety over unmet needs will dissipate.

2. You fear the future.

The spirit of mammon cannot control the future; only God can and His plans for us are good, not evil. We should never fear the future because God extends His hand toward us and supplies our every need according to Philippians 4:19. We can trust God to take care of us (Psalm 104:28). Trusting in Him shuts down the spirit of mammon.

3. **You have unbelief in your heart.**

Mammon tells you that God's ways are foolish and outdated, and causes unbelief to take root in your spirit. It stops us from tithing and giving, or convinces us that tithing and giving offerings puts us under the Law of Moses instead of under grace. This is simply not true. We give tithes and offerings because we love God, not because we are afraid we will be cursed if we don't. Mammon also brings with it a spirit of envy, and causes us to lie and cheat to get ahead financially. God often uses possessions as a test; and how we respond to someone else being blessed indicates the condition of our hearts (Deuteronomy 5:21). Our faith in God's ability to take care of us is going to be demonstrated by our corresponding actions. Giving even when it appears we don't have enough is a way to overcome unbelief and strengthen that faith.

4. **It brings disobedience in our lives.**

We are God's stewards and He wants us to prosper and be generous, but mammon wants us to be selfish. God wants to bless us and free us to obey His Word; mammon wants to bring us into a curse through disobedience to God's instructions. Whatever God tells us to do has a blessing attached to it, but what mammon tries to influence us to do has a curse attached to it.

5. **Mammon derides us for trusting God.**

The Pharisees derided Jesus when He was explaining about money (Luke 16:14, 15), and people still have a tendency to do this when the topic of finances is brought up in the church. Don't be surprised if you face persecution for following God's instructions in the financial arena or embracing Jesus' teachings on the subject. Also, don't allow yourself to deride and scorn others who embrace Jesus' teachings on money. When you do this, the spirit of mammon is in operation.

6. It causes us to determine success by how much money we make.

We live in a society and culture that places achievement and financial success above everything else. Real success is fulfilling God's will for our lives. Mammon wants us to live as consumers, not stewards. It gives us an entitlement mentality, and tells us we can live beyond our financial means, but then leaves us. Don't buy into mammon's false message of financial obsession "by any means necessary."

There is a way to remove yourself from mammon's death grip once you realize it has gained a foothold in your life. Repent for allowing money to have your heart and soul, and acknowledge God as your only source. Ask Him to show you what He wants you to do with your financial resources and obey Him. By rebelling against the spirit of mammon, you send a message to the devil that you cannot be controlled or manipulated by greed. In demonstrating responsibility with the least (money), you position yourself to be a steward of the many blessings of the kingdom of God that rightfully belong to you.

Study Questions

1. True or False: The Bible is the primary way to learn how to manage your finances.

2. What happens when we don't trust God with our money? _____

3. What is mammon's agenda? _____

4. Mammon hides behind _____.

5. What did Jesus teach about money in the kingdom of God? _____

6. What is the Aramaic translation of "mammon"? _____

7. Mammon wants to bring us under a _____ through _____.

8. True or False: Persecution is attached to discussing money in the church.

9. What does our society prize above all else? _____

10. How can you remove yourself from mammon's grip? _____

SCRIPTURE REFERENCES

Luke 16:10-15

Matthew 4:8-10

Luke 19:1-26

Luke 12:16-21

Philippians 4:19

Psalm 104:28

Deuteronomy 5:21

CHAPTER SIX
The Tactics of Mammon

When it comes to understanding how the spirit of mammon moves and operates, it is vital to identify its tactics. One of the ways mammon tries to attack is through the spirit of fear, which manifests in many Christians' lives as the fear of having material possessions. So many believers are afraid to acquire money because they think that it will cause problems for them. However, money is not responsible for the bad things that happen in people's lives; their wrong relationship with money is the problem. As Christian people on a mission to impact this world for the kingdom of God, we need wealth in order to effectively minister to others in the physical realm. Many people take the emphasis off of money for fear of becoming consumed with it and theorize that the wealth of God is only spiritual, but the truth is that heaven is a place where the streets are paved with gold. The lesson here is that money isn't the problem, but the spirit that can be attached to money is. The spirit of mammon is responsible for the fall of Babylon and is running rampant in society today as well. Every day we are in a battle between choosing God's way of doing things and the way of mammon. We must learn how this spirit operates, uncover its maneuvers, and choose to trust God.

Again, one of the weapons mammon uses against people is the spirit of fear. It does not want the truth to come out and it does not want to be exposed. In Jesus' day, the Pharisees scoffed at Jesus' teachings because they were greedy and afraid that His message would cause them to lose money. For example, Jesus taught that he who is faithful in the least (referring to financial matters) is also faithful in much, and he who is unjust in the least is also unjust in much (Luke 16:10-14). He let the people know that no servant can serve two masters; either you will hate the one and despise the other, or hold to the one and despise the other. His message was simply this: you cannot serve God and mammon. The religious leaders who were greedy, money-hungry, and covetous heard these things and constantly came against Jesus.

This same spirit that the Pharisees operated in can be seen today in many churches that do not want to talk about money matters. So many preachers will not talk about anything having to do with the financial realm for fear of what people will say or think. Tradition causes people to be afraid to give, but the Word of God tells us that the traditions of men make the Scriptures of no effect (Mark 7:13). The spirit of mammon not only causes us to hold on to money, but also to hold on to bad traditions in every other area of our lives.

First John 2:15-17 gives us a great antidote to the spirit of mammon: *"Love not the world, neither the things that are in the world. If any man love the world, the love of the Father is not in him. For all that is in the world, the lust of the flesh, and the lust of the eyes, and the pride of life, is not of the Father, but is of the world. And the world passeth away, and the lust thereof: but he that doeth the will of God abideth for ever."* The "world" in this context is referring to the world's systems, mindsets, norms, and values that do not take the Scriptures into consideration. The attitude of the world is that whatever the majority is doing is right. The "flesh" is a mindset that goes against God's word. The lust of the eyes causes us to want whatever others have, and pride refuses to submit to God's will, preferring instead to do whatever it wants to do at the moment. This Scripture is basically alluding to the same thing Jesus said in Luke 16:13: your allegiance cannot be to God and the spirit of the world, which is the spirit of mammon.

The spirit of mammon can be easily identified by the fact that it *always* opposes God's will. For example, in the book of Matthew, Peter began to rebuke Jesus in an attempt to stop Him from going to the cross, but Jesus turned to Peter and said, "Get behind me, Satan, you are an offense to me" (Matthew 16:22, 23). Peter's attempt to stop Jesus from fulfilling the assignment that He had come to the earth to do was an indication that he was under the influence of the demonic spirit of mammon. When someone or something attempts to distract you from what God has said in His Word or spoken to you, know the spirit of mammon is coming against you. Follow in the footsteps of Jesus and rebuke it immediately.

DON'T CLING TO RICHES

Mammon is the enemy of God and the enemy of those who follow Christ. It wants to use people and then destroy them. We see another example of the spirit of mammon in operation in the lives of Ananias and Sapphira, two members of the early church who sold land and kept back part of the money for themselves. They were completely possessed by this demonic spirit:

> But a certain man named Ananias, with Sapphira his wife, sold a possession, And kept back part of the price, his wife also being privy to it, and brought a certain part, and laid it at the apostle's feet. But Peter said, Ananias, why hath Satan filled thine heart to lie to the Holy Ghost, and to keep back part of the price of the

land? Whiles it remained, was it not thine own? and after it was sold, was it not in thine own power? why hast thou conceived this thing in thine heart? thou hast not lied unto men, but unto God. And Ananias hearing these words fell down, and gave up the ghost: and great fear came on all them that heard these things. And the young men arose, wound him up, and carried him out, and buried him. And it was about the space of three hours after, when his wife, not knowing what was done, came in. And Peter answered unto her, Tell me whether ye sold the land for so much? And she said, Yea, for so much. Then Peter said unto her, How is it that ye have agreed together to tempt the Spirit of the Lord? behold, the feet of them which have buried thy husband are at the door, and shall carry thee out. Then fell she down straightway at his feet, and yielded up the ghost: and the young men came in, and found her dead, and, carrying her forth, buried her by her husband. And great fear came upon all the church, and upon as many as heard these things (Acts 5:1-11).

Ananias and Sapphira were motivated by the spirit of mammon, which led them to keep money that should have been given to the church, and then lie about it. In the end, their love of money and their willingness to yield to the spirit of mammon rather than the Spirit of God resulted in their demise.

The love of money is fueled by the spirit of mammon and is the root of all evil. Ananias and Sapphira exemplify First Timothy 6:10 that talks about those who have given in to the love of money, erred from the faith, and pierced themselves through with many sorrows. Money itself is not the enemy, but the spirit behind it is what makes it good or bad. For this reason, we must understand that it is God's will for us to have money, but we aren't to trust in it (1 Timothy 6:17). *"Wealth and riches shall be in his house: and his righteousness endureth for ever*" (Psalm 112:3). If God controls the money, there will be no downside to possessing it (Proverbs 10:22). If you think it is not God's will for His people to have money, you simply don't understand His heart. He just doesn't want possessions to have you. We don't have to be afraid of having money when we have a balanced understanding of God's purpose and plan for bringing material resources into our lives.

MONEY IS GOD'S WILL IN THE LIFE OF A BELIEVER

Like any other thing in the kingdom of God, we must *believe* God wants us to prosper if we are going to walk in His plan for our lives. His plan for us includes finances and resources. It is completely okay to have wealth and riches, as long as we stay in the will of God and don't allow the spirit of mammon to get a foothold. The Scriptures give us some guidelines to help keep us on track.

Philippians 4:5 says, "*Let our moderation be known unto all men. The Lord is at hand.*" When God blesses us richly, those who misunderstand His Word in this area will think that "moderation" is referring to not being excessive. They take this Scripture out of context. The Greek definition of the word, *moderation*, is "unselfishness, consideration, and forbearance." One way that we guard against the spirit of mammon is to cultivate an attitude of unselfishness when it comes to our finances. We are to consider others and how God wants us to bless other people with the resources that He brings into our hands.

Another blueprint for avoiding the traps of mammon can be found in Luke 12:15: "*And he said unto them, Take heed, and beware of covetousness: for a man's life consisteth not in the abundance of the things which he possesseth.*" Jesus told the parable of the rich man who pulled down his barns to build new ones to contain all that he had, instead of giving to others. God referred to this man as a fool because, while he had laid up treasures for himself in this earthly realm, he was spiritually and morally bankrupt.

Life is not about collecting stuff. Jesus warned against greed, which opens the door to the spirit of mammon causing destruction. However, there is nothing wrong with having nice things as long as we do not let the spirit of mammon control our thinking in this area. Fools do not acknowledge God; they choose mammon instead (Psalm 14:1). Sometimes we stray so far from God that, when we listen to mammon, we think God left us. The truth is that He will never leave us or forsake us (Deuteronomy 31:6; Hebrews 13:5). It is simply up to us to return to Him and commit ourselves to trusting Him, not ourselves or the spirit in the world.

The spirit of mammon can never bring lasting happiness or fulfillment to a person's life; it can only bring destruction and desolation when everything is all said and done. God desires for us to use our resources wisely and ultimately to build His kingdom. We have to reject the spirit of fear that mammon uses to try to keep us from having what God wants us to have, while also rejecting the temptation to give money the wrong position in our lives. Trusting God is the key. In developing our trust in God, alone, for our financial provision and increase, we demonstrate that we can handle all that He wants to give us and do in our lives.

Study Questions

1. One of the ways mammon tries to attack is through the spirit of _____.

2. What is one of the ways mammon manifests as fear in a Christian's life? _____

3. True or False: Money is responsible for bad things happening in people's lives.

4. Why did the Pharisees scoff at Jesus' teachings on financial matters?
   _____
   _____

5. The spirit of mammon causes us to hold on to bad _____.

6. What is the "world"? _____

7. How can you easily identify that the spirit of mammon is in operation? _____

8. Why did Ananias and Sapphira do what they did? _____
   _____

9. True or False: Moderation refers to us not being excessive with our finances.

10. True or False: It is God's will for Christians to have money.

SCRIPTURE REFERENCES

Luke 16:10-14

Mark 7:13

1 John 2:15-17

Matthew 16:22, 23

Acts 5:1-11

1 Timothy 6:10, 17

Psalm 112:3

Proverbs 10:22

Philippians 4:5

Luke 12:13-21

Psalm 14:1

Deuteronomy 31:6

Hebrews 13:5

Psalm 23:6

CHAPTER SEVEN
The Operation of the Spirit of Mammon

The Operation of the Spirit of Mammon

The enemy has a specific strategy he uses to cause damage in people's lives: hiding himself and his operation from our view. When we are ignorant of Satan's devices, we can easily be overtaken by him. This is his number one goal, but God has given us all the tools we need to overcome the enemy's deceptive tactics. The spirit of mammon is a subtle, sneaky demon that hides from us and tries to disguise itself as the spiritual voice we hear in religion. Most churches are possessed with this spirit and have no idea they are under its influence. It always rises up against the Word of God concerning money and a host of other issues. When the subjects of finances and trust are preached, those who are controlled by the spirit of mammon tend to reject the message. However, Jesus taught some very powerful lessons about money. He always discussed it in relation to trusting God. This is really what this battle with the spirit of mammon is about—trust. God wants us to trust in Him and not money. Uncovering the spirit of mammon includes understanding how it operates so that we can defeat it.

One clue that the spirit of mammon is present is when we verbally confess that we trust God, but pull back from trusting Him with our finances. We are deceived if we believe we can trust Him with the greater things of the kingdom of God and cannot trust Him with our money, which Jesus refers to as the *least*. In light of what God says about finances in His kingdom, we must decide for ourselves whether we are being influenced by God or mammon.

In revealing the operation of the spirit of mammon, the thing to always remember is that the spirit of mammon directly opposes everything God teaches. It will talk to us and tell us things that contradict the Word of God. For example, mammon says, "buy and keep," but God says, "sow and reap." These different messages let you know how mammon tries to get you to have twisted thinking as it relates to money. Mammon is looking for servants; it wants to rule our lives and take God's place. It deceives us and then leaves us in a pit by ourselves. God picks us up out of the pit, puts our feet on solid ground, and never leaves us. Mammon is selfish, but God is generous. Mammon tries to insulate us from life's problems by trusting in money, or it causes us to dwell on our problems. It tries to confuse us about God's principles. It is not a source of security in any way, shape, or form; God is.

Mammon was behind Peter's attempt to stop Jesus from fulfilling God's redemptive plan for mankind when he rebuked Jesus (Matthew 16:21-23). Jesus was speaking of the will of God concerning the events to come and Peter was under the influence of a crafty, deceptive demon. He shows us that if we are not careful about what we say, we can unwittingly speak something that is outside of God's will. We need to know God's Word well enough to recognize when the spirit of mammon tries to influence us away from the truth. Mammon hides behind religion, and takes advantage of ignorance about God and His Word. It even encourages us to sing songs that contradict God's promises. We don't have to beg God never to leave us because He promises that He won't (Hebrews 13:5).

The spirit of mammon was also at work in the life of Judas Iscariot, prompting him to meet with the chief priests to discuss how he would betray Jesus for thirty pieces of silver. Through the spirit of mammon, the transaction was made and the Pharisees agreed to pay Judas to betray Jesus (Luke 22:1-6). Judas was motivated by the devil to establish a covenant to serve mammon. See, mammon causes us to trust in money and do something that will eventually come back to us to destroy our lives. It always leaves us at the end of our rope, just like it did Judas who ended up hanging himself after betraying Jesus. You always come up short when you put your trust in anything other than God.

Though the spirit of mammon consistently lies to us and takes us deeper and deeper into a place of despair and darkness, the Spirit of God is faithful and true to us all the time. We can trust in God and His ability to take care of us. Every act of evil is rooted in the spirit of mammon and, when we love money, we are demonstrating that we trust in it more than we trust God. To avoid falling into the bondage of mammon, there are three things that we need to understand about this spirit. First, it tells us that it can protect us from our problems and that money is the solution to everything. While it is true that we need money to live in this world, money is not the solution to everything. It cannot buy health, loving relationships, or deliverance. Many people have money but are still suffering in areas of their lives that cannot be rectified with money. Mammon cannot give us the security we seek in this life.

Second, it gives the illusion of providing things that only God can provide. Everyone wants to live a prosperous life, but true prosperity includes intangible things that cannot be acquired with money. God is the only one who can give us true peace in this life. Money can't do that. The fruit of the Spirit and the gifts of the Spirit cannot be secured through the spirit of mammon. Trusting in God for everything that concerns us is the only answer to the spirit of mammon attempting to worm its way into our lives.

Third, it causes fear and tells us that we do not have enough money or wealth, regardless of what we actually possess. The lying spirit of mammon wants to constantly highlight what we don't have, rather than allowing us to focus on the blessings that we do have at the moment. It tells us that if we could just get more money, then all of our issues would go away. It causes us to overlook the things that God has provided for us and seek more and more gratification through things other than God. Mammon is a destructive spirit that robs people of the blessings of God.

Overcoming the fear of lack is something that every believer will have to do, which is why God will allow us to experience situations and circumstances that force us to trust Him. He wants us to remain in a position of dependence on Him for all of our needs. Jesus asked His disciples if they lacked anything when He sent them out (Luke 22:35, 36). They didn't have money, shoes, or any other supplies with them and yet they were well taken care of. Jesus' goal here was to point out to His disciples that they would lack nothing if they trusted Him. His message was to let them know that when they pass the test of trusting in God, they can be trusted with more money and other possessions.

God's ultimate goal is to teach us that He is the source of our prosperity, not ourselves. No matter how hard we toil or how smart we think we are, at the end of the day, God is the one who gives us the power to get wealth. He is the source of our provision. The person who trusts in his or her riches will inevitably fall, but the righteous will flourish like a healthy branch (Proverbs 11:28). When we trust money, it will let us down, but when we trust God, we will never be let down. Purpose in your heart to trust God for everything in your life, from your health to your finances, and watch Him do exceeding, abundantly above all that you could ever ask or think!

Study Questions

1. How does the enemy get away with his operations? _____
   _____

2. What tends to happen when the spirit of mammon is controlling a particular church? _____

3. What is the battle with the spirit of mammon about? _____
   _____

4. How does God determine if we can be trusted with great things in His kingdom? _____

5. The spirit of mammon says, "buy and keep," but God says, "_____ _____ and _____."

6. Mammon is looking for _____.

7. True or False: Money is the solution to everything in life.

8. What is the danger of giving yourself over to the spirit of mammon?
   _____

9. What three things does the spirit of mammon tell people?
   _____
   _____

10. What is God's ultimate goal? _____
    _____

SCRIPTURE REFERENCES

Matthew 16:21-23

Hebrews 13:5

Luke 22:1-6, 35, 36

Proverbs 11:28

CHAPTER EIGHT
The Sneaky Spirit of Mammon

One of the reasons a snake is so dangerous is because it is very subtle and sneaky. It can inflict great damage because it is quiet and moves in such a way that you are not aware it is even in your vicinity. Similar to the way a snake moves, mammon is a very sneaky spirit that has the potential to do great damage in people's lives. It is an evil spirit whose main goal is to steal, kill, and destroy. It readily attaches itself to money and does its best to get us to trust wealth more than we do God. It always contradicts the Word of God and attempts to persuade us to develop a wrong relationship with the financial realm. When mammon is controlling a person's life, compromise and deception are present. One of the most notable manifestations of the spirit of mammon was in the life of Judas, who betrayed Jesus for money (Matthew 26:14-16). Entire nations have fallen under the influence of this foul spirit, which aims to seduce us with lies, use us, destroy our lives, and then leave us broken. As Christians, we must be careful not to allow ourselves to be lured away from the Spirit of God and fall under the rule of the spirit of mammon. Studying what the Bible says about money will open our eyes to the work of this spirit so that we can recognize it for what it is.

The spirit of mammon has one goal: to fool us into serving it instead of God. Because everything in the kingdom of God is connected to trusting God, if the devil can get us to serve him through the wicked spirit of mammon, we will lose our ability to be effective representatives for Christ. Jesus told His disciples the parable of the steward who was dismissed from his position because he had squandered all of his master's money. He concluded the parable by telling them that no servant can serve two masters; they will hate one and despise the other. The truth is that you cannot serve God and mammon (Luke 16:1-13).

The context of this parable focuses solely on a steward who was unfaithful with money, which Jesus actually refers to as the least in the kingdom of God. If we can be trusted with money, we can be trusted with much more important things from a spiritual perspective—healing, deliverance, and the spiritual gifts of God, to name a few. Some people believe that Jesus doesn't want anything to do with the financial realm or that Christianity and money should not mix, but God cares deeply about people's relationship with money and Jesus wants us to handle our resources wisely and skillfully.

When we choose to honor God, it means that He carries weight and holds a high value in our lives. Proverbs 3:9, 10 says to honor the Lord with the firstfruits of our increase and our barns will be filled with plenty. To honor God with our substance is to put Him first in our finances rather than making Him an afterthought. For example, we tithe before we pay our bills and buy things for ourselves. We pray and seek God about where He would have us to sow our seed first. The Word says that the love of money is the root of all evil, and that those who are overtaken with the desire to pursue money end up damaging themselves (1 Timothy 6:10). The spirit of mammon wants to steal, kill, and destroy our lives by getting us to love money, just like Judas did. The end result of his greed and lust for money was that he killed himself (Matthew 27:3-5). Those who allow mammon to control them will always experience destruction. The love of money is revealed when we trust in it more than we do God. This indicates a wrong relationship with the material realm.

AVOIDING MAMMON'S PLANS TO DESTROY

When you sense the enemy moving in for the kill by enticing you to trust in money more than you do God, remind yourself that mammon's plans for you are always the opposite of God's will for your life. Wherever your treasure is, there will your heart be also (Matthew 6:21). The test that determines where your heart is, is found when you examine how and where you spend your money. Through demonic influence, the spirit of mammon seeks to control people's lives and keep them in bondage.

The spirit of mammon wants to attach itself to money but it is not limited only to money. Any attempt to derail God's will in any area comes from the spirit of mammon. For example, when Jesus had to rebuke Peter for trying to stop Him from going to the cross, the spirit of mammon was at work. *"From that time forth began Jesus to shew unto his disciples, how that he must go unto Jerusalem, and suffer many things of the elders and chief priests and scribes, and be killed, and be raised again the third day. Then Peter took him, and began to rebuke him, saying, Be it far from thee, Lord: this shall not be unto thee. But he turned, and said unto Peter, Get thee behind me, Satan: thou art an offence unto me: for thou savourest not the things that be of God, but those that be of men"* (Matthew 16:21-23). Jesus had announced God's plan to the disciples, but Peter was under demonic influence when he rebuked Jesus. What he was saying sounded like it was coming from a place of concern, but it was really motivated by the spirit of mammon, which always stands in opposition to God's plan. We must be able to recognize this spirit so that we can resist it (Ephesians 6:12).

There are three characteristics that we need to understand about mammon in order to avoid falling into bondage to this spirit. First, mammon tells us that it can protect us from our problems and that money is the solution. Second, it appears to provide things that only God can give, such as security, significance, identity, power, freedom, and self-esteem. Third, mammon causes fear. It tells us we do not have enough money, no matter how much we do have. It is a spirit of lies and deception that tries to entice people into going against their consciences in pursuit of the almighty dollar.

If we are going to gain the victory over the spirit of mammon, it is going to require placing our trust in God and meditating on His Word so that we can become established in His promises and in the finished works of Jesus Christ. There is nothing that Jesus has not made available to us. By putting our confidence in what He has done, we move away from self-effort and the pride that comes from trying to do things in our own ability.

The spirit of mammon is destructive. It gains entry into our lives when we take our focus off of Jesus. By allowing Him to maintain the highest position in our lives and making a quality decision to honor God with our finances even when we don't feel like doing so, we are rebelling against the spirit of mammon and preventing it from getting a foothold in our lives. Take note of when you feel tempted to spend your money on yourself before sowing into the things of God. Become aware of the voice of fear that tells you to hoard what you have instead of giving a portion of it to someone in need. By practicing intentional giving and fixing your heart and mind on God's ability and not your own, you can overcome the subtle spirit of mammon and walk in the fullness of what God has prepared for you not only financially, but in every area of your life.

Study Questions

1. What is the mission of the spirit of mammon? _____
   _____

2. What does the spirit of mammon have a tendency to attach itself to?
   _____

3. True or False: The spirit of mammon always contradicts the Word of God.

4. You cannot serve _____ and _____.

5. What is considered the least in the kingdom of God? _____

6. True or False: Christianity and the financial realm should not mix.

7. What does it mean to honor God? _____
   _____

8. What are some of the things mammon promises to provide?
   _____

9. How do we gain victory over the spirit of mammon?
   _____

10. How does the spirit of mammon gain entry into our lives?
    _____

SCRIPTURE REFERENCES

Matthew 26:14-16

Luke 16:1-13

Proverbs 3:9, 10

1 Timothy 6:10

Matthew 27:3-5

Matthew 6:21

Matthew 16:21-23

Ephesians 6:12

CHAPTER NINE
Uncovering the Spirit of Mammon

If there is one spirit that will absolutely steal, kill, and destroy everything God desires to do in your life, it is the spirit of mammon. This demonic spirit is very pervasive and subtle, and it can be difficult to detect unless we remain vigilant against it. It wants to attach itself to money and it tries to persuade us to trust money instead of God. Wealth and riches are a part of every believer's inheritance in the kingdom of God, but wealth and riches cannot buy healing, deliverance, grace, or other blessings because *trust* is the currency of God's kingdom. We have to trust God with *every* aspect of our lives, including our financial and material resources. Whether we are trustworthy with the things of God is demonstrated by how we handle money, which God considers the least important thing in His kingdom. We can choose to let the spirit of mammon dictate what we do with money, or allow the Spirit of God to direct us in this area. If we fail to choose God's instructions, by default, the spirit of mammon will govern our lives. Now, more than ever, we must be careful about what spirit influences us when it comes to the financial realm. Faithfulness with money will determine if we can be faithful in the greater areas of our lives.

The Bible talks a lot about money and for good reason. In the parable about the unjust steward who mismanaged his master's money, the steward was dismissed from his position. Despite that, his master commended him for doing wisely. Jesus asked His disciples who would commit to their trust true riches if they had not been faithful with unrighteous mammon (Luke 16:1-13). The primary lesson Jesus was teaching through this parable was the value of wise money management. The steward was forward-thinking enough to cut deals with the people who owed his master money, hoping they would do favors for him when he was no longer a steward. The end result was that the master commended him. God wants us to view money as a tool to take care of our futures rather than something we become consumed with just to take care of our present circumstances. The mindset of the believer must mirror this way of thinking.

It is also important to remember that money not only impacts the present and the future, but also eternity. If we have done the right thing with money, when we die we will meet people we helped financially, and they will appreciate what we did for them (Luke 16:9). The "least" that Jesus referred to in verse ten is money. While most of us have been convinced that the highest exertion of our faith is reserved for bringing finances into our hands, this is actually not what the Word teaches. If we can master money right where we are, and commit to being givers in our current financial situation, we demonstrate our level of trust in God. Faith in God alone means we don't wait to give when our incomes are bigger, but that we give now, and from a cheerful heart.

UNCOVERING THE SPIRIT OF MAMMON

There are some key facts that we need to understand about the spirit of mammon. First, it is a spirit that is in direct contrast to the Spirit of God. It is the spirit of the world and the spirit of Satan himself. Mammon says, "buy and keep," while God says, "sow and reap." Mammon says, "cheat and steal," while God says, "give and receive." The entire system of mammon is in opposition to God's way of doing things, which is why it is so dangerous to get caught up in mammon's traps.

Mammon wants us to compromise our values and sacrifice our very character for money. It wants to rule our lives and bring us into bondage. The spirit of mammon influenced the prodigal son, who left home and made poor decisions because of money. That same spirit influenced the elder son, who became angry when he learned that his younger brother had returned and received favor from their father after living a reckless life (Luke 15:11-32). You see, mammon is all about self-centeredness, which ultimately leads to bitterness. It promises to give us things that only God can provide. Mammon is selfish, while God is generous. Mammon talks to us when we are trying to give to God and tries to convince us that our money could be better used for something else. It is the spirit behind the hesitance to tithe when you have a bill that is due. It is the feeling of holding on to what little you have instead of sowing it into someone else's life.

The story of the rich young ruler is a prime example of what happens when a person's life is under the influence of the spirit of mammon. Matthew 19:16-22 says:

> And, behold, one came and said unto him, Good Master, what good thing shall I do, that I may have eternal life? And he said unto him, Why callest thou me good? there is none good but one, that is, God: but if thou wilt enter into life, keep the commandments. He saith unto him, Which? Jesus said, Thou shalt do no murder, Thou shalt not commit adultery, Thou shalt not steal, Thou shalt not bear false witness, Honour thy father and thy mother: and, Thou shalt love thy neighbor as thyself. The young man saith unto him, All these things have I kept from

my youth up: what lack I yet? Jesus said unto him, If thou wilt be perfect, go and sell that thou hast, and give to the poor, and thou shalt have treasure in heaven: and come and follow me. But when the young man heard that saying, he went away sorrowful: for he had great possessions.

This young man's attachment to his material possessions was driven by the spirit of mammon. As a result, he turned down the greatest ministry opportunity of his life. That's what mammon will do to you; it will have you believing the lie that your materials are more valuable than obeying God. You will find yourself leaving the promises of God for a life that will never satisfy you.

Mammon doesn't just come by itself, but it brings three other destructive spirits with it: pride, greed, and poverty. Any time you see these things manifesting in a person's life, you can be certain that the spirit of mammon is involved. The spirit of poverty will make us ashamed of the blessings of God and want to shrink away from showing the world what God is doing in our lives, especially in the financial arena. The spirit of pride will not acknowledge God for His blessings, but will want to take credit for the results through self-effort. The spirit of greed will cause us to hold on to everything we have and seek even more. Mammon also causes us to get into a spirit of idolatry, which is where we replace God with something or someone else. We are told to honor God and give Him first place in our lives; but the spirit of mammon wants to replace God's position in our hearts and turn honor into dishonor. All together, these spiritual forces wreak havoc in the life of a believer and keep him or her trapped in a life of toil and destruction.

The objective of the spirit of mammon is ultimately to steal our trust in God. We must vigilantly guard against this because our trust is what connects us to the finished works of Jesus. Proverbs 3:5-9 instructs us to trust in the Lord with all our heart and lean not to our own understanding. When we trust in the Lord, He directs our paths. We are to turn away from being wise in our own eyes, fear God, and depart from evil. We are to honor God with our money, and give Him the best of all of our increase. This is the essence of what it means to be a Christian. It is about trusting and relying on God for *everything* in our lives. We must trust God instead of money. Mammon, on the other hand, does not want us to acknowledge Him.

The spirit of mammon is extremely unfaithful, while attempting to get us to be faithful to it at all costs. When it is finished with us, however, it will leave us desolate. It does not offer us the same commitment that God does. God promises to never leave or forsake us (Deuteronomy 31:6; Hebrews 13:5), but mammon will always abandon us after taking everything we have.

God never talks about trust without talking about money, which is why trusting Him *with* our money is so very important. Jesus commended the widow woman who gave the little that she had because she trusted God. We can look at her as an example of what pleases the Lord. When we give, even when we don't have much, God looks at it like we are giving a huge amount of money to His kingdom. We show Him that we can be entrusted with greater riches and responsibilities in the kingdom of God when our allegiance to Him is the only allegiance that exists.

Study Questions

1. What does the spirit of mammon try to persuade us to do? _____
   _____

2. _____ is the currency of God's kingdom.

3. What are a part of every believer's inheritance in the kingdom of God? _____

4. What happens when we fail to trust God with our money?
   _____

5. True or False: Money's impact is not just on the earth.

6. How does God want us to view money? _____
   _____

7. True or False: When we die, we will meet the people we impacted financially on the earth.

8. Mammon is _____ and God is _____.

9. What is the objective of the spirit of mammon? _____
   _____

10. God promises to direct our _____ when we trust Him and not ourselves.

SCRIPTURE REFERENCES

Luke 16:1-13

Luke 15:11-32

Matthew 19:16-22

Proverbs 3:5-9

Deuteronomy 31:6

Hebrews 13:5

CHAPTER TEN
The Giving-Trust Connection

As believers, the Word of God is our final authority. It is vital that we read and meditate on it regularly so that we can understand how God wants us to live. If we are to remain spiritually strong, we must surround ourselves with other believers and fellowship through church attendance. Doing so gives us the spiritual sustenance we need in our daily lives. One of the things we can learn from the Word of God is the importance of giving. In fact, giving is one of the most important topics that we should get hold of in the Bible. God wants to shower us with His favor and blessings at all times, but whether we benefit from His promises depends largely on whether we believe what the Bible says about being givers. Giving activates a spiritual law of seedtime and harvest that puts us in a position for prophecies to come to pass in our lives. It goes hand in hand with reflecting the nature of Jesus to the world. When we say we trust Him, giving is an expression of that trust. To say we trust God and not give of our resources is to live a contradictory life.

Financial giving is one of the main ways we express our trust in God. We cannot say we believe and not trust God because trust is the currency of the kingdom of God. Money can't *buy* God's favor, but when we put all of our trust in God we activate His blessings in our lives. When God asks us to give of our resources, it is not about the money; it is a heart issue. Trusting God enough to give of what we have causes us to experience blessings. The things we need and desire will inevitably show up in our lives when we trust God.

Deuteronomy 15:10, *ESV*, says, *"You shall give to him freely, and your heart shall not be grudging when you give to him, because for this the* L*ord* *your God will bless you in all your work and in all that you undertake."* When we give to God, He will bless us; this is a guarantee. However, when we give to God, it should be because we really want to, not because we feel obligated to do so. God loves it when our giving comes from a cheerful heart, not a grudging one.

Again, God will bless us when we give to Him; it activates the spiritual principle of sowing and reaping. This blessing empowers us to be successful in every area of our lives and it makes us rich. You see, when God blesses you, there is no sorrow attached (Proverbs 10:22). That's the difference between a blessing that comes from Him versus something you received from the devil or through your own self-effort. This blessing will cause abundance, not just financially, but in all other areas of your life, as well. In fact, abundance is the hallmark of the giver (John 10:10). Jesus came to *give* and, not only that, to give us the abundant life.

BEING GENEROUS

So, what is the heart-condition God is looking for when it comes to our giving? He wants to see generosity. It is possible to give outwardly but have a heart that is holding back. When this is your heart-condition, you are not giving from a heart that reflects God's nature. He is a generous, abundant, lavish giver. The generous giver doesn't take into consideration what is in his or her bank account before giving; he or she just gives. Similarly, because everyone is blessed in varying degrees, what may look like a large offering for one person may not really be a generous gift to another. To whom much is given, much is required. For example, a millionaire giving a $5,000 offering is not a sacrifice, but a person who only has $100 in his or her bank account would be giving generously if their offering was $75. God always looks to see what we give in proportion to what we have, and the attitude in which we give.

"There is that scattereth, and yet increaseth; and there is that withholdeth more than is meet, but it tendeth to poverty. The liberal soul shall be made fat: and he that watereth shall be watered also himself" (Proverbs 11:24, 25). God always provides us with opportunities to give but we must recognize those opportunities and take advantage of them. Giving generously from your resources actually brings more increase into your hands, versus withholding what you have and slowing down the flow of increase. God promises to bless those who give.

Giving generously and in the right spirit is pleasing to God, which is why our motive is always the most important thing. First Chronicles 29:9 says, *"Then the people rejoiced, for that they offered willingly, because with perfect heart they offered willingly to the* LORD: *and David the king also rejoiced with great joy."* When we truly trust God, we find ourselves wanting to give. Giving is a characteristic of love and our job is to love by being givers. We should want to help those who need assistance and reach out to those who are hurting. The book of Proverbs promises blessings for giving to the poor and helping the needy. This is actually the responsibility of every believer and shows that we honor God and the people He loves and wants to help (Proverbs 22:9; 28:27).

When we give, we have to be sure that we don't allow self-righteousness or a haughty spirit to set in. We aren't supposed to brag about our good deeds or try to take credit for what we do. Giving to build ourselves up is the wrong motivation. We should give because we truly are givers from the heart and are walking in the character of Christ, who lives in us.

Why should we be givers as sons of God? Because God is the source of everything we have! How can we not give as a reflection of His character when everything that comes into our hands comes from Him in the first place? We are not the source of our prosperity or resources; we are simply stewards of all that He owns. God gave to us so that we could share what we have with others. Whatever we decided in our hearts to give is what we should give, and we should do so without reluctance. This is the heart of a cheerful giver and it pleases God.

Remember that you can honor the Lord with whatever you have, no matter what your financial condition is. So many people say they are going to give once they acquire more resources, but the true test is whether you give when you don't have the means just yet. The Word instructs us to honor the Lord with our substance so that our storehouses will overflow (Proverbs 3:9, 10). It does not say, "Honor the Lord when you have a whole lot of money in the bank." This Scripture refers to our financial resources. It lets us know that we are to honor God with whatever we have. To honor something or someone means that it carries weight in our lives and we make it our first priority. When we give, we prove to ourselves that God carries more weight than cash. We should never trust our money or material possessions more than we trust God (1 Timothy 6:10).

Faith to give, and give big, comes from continually studying the Word of God and hearing the truth about giving preached over and over again. The more we receive the Word about trusting God through giving, the more we will have the confidence to step out on God's instructions and give, no matter our circumstances or situation in life. As we do, we will activate the blessings and favor of God. Trust is demonstrated by our willingness to give. By becoming cheerful givers, we can expect an abundant harvest to flood our lives.

Study Questions

1. Why is God so big on giving? _____
   _____

2. True or False: Giving financially generates abundant blessings.

3. Money can't buy God's _____.

4. What is the difference between the blessing of God and what comes from Satan or self-effort? _____
   _____

5. The blessing will cause _____ in our lives.

6. What is the heart-condition God is looking for when we give?
   _____

7. True or False: You can give outwardly while inwardly holding back.

8. How does the generous giver think? _____
   _____

9. Why should we be givers? _____
   _____

10. How do we develop the faith to become generous givers? _____
    _____

SCRIPTURE REFERENCES

Deuteronomy 15:10, *ESV*

Proverbs 10:22

John 10:10

Proverbs 11:24, 25

1 Chronicles 29:9, 14

Proverbs 22:9

Proverbs 28:27

Proverbs 3:9, 10

1 Timothy 6:10

Deuteronomy 16:17

Proverbs 21:26

Matthew 6:3, 4

2 Corinthians 9:7

2 Corinthians 8:12

CHAPTER ELEVEN
Your Giving Is an Expression of Your Trust

Did you know that your attitude toward financial giving, and whether you actually give financially, are demonstrations of the degree to which you trust God? When we examine the relationship between finances and trust, there are several questions to consider: who should give, why and how we should give, to whom we should give, and what will happen when we give. Every Christian should be a giver because it is a privilege and a responsibility for those who have received the gift of eternal life. We give because of our love and sense of thanksgiving for what Jesus did. We should give with a cheerful heart because we want to, not because we have to. We should give to the poor and to ministries that help those in need. When we do this, God promises to bless us. Money is neither good nor bad; it is simply a tool that equips us to help others. Money is the least important issue in the kingdom of God, and if we can trust Him with our finances, we can trust Him with all other aspects of our lives.

One of the fundamental principles that we have to understand about giving is that it is never about the money. When God looks at our giving, He wants us to prove to ourselves that we trust in Him. In Luke 16:1-13, we see Jesus telling the story of the rich man whose steward was accused of stealing his goods. The rich man told the steward that he could no longer be in that position. The steward then called his lord's debtors and settled the debts by having them pay only a part of what they owed. The rich man commended the steward for acting wisely, and Jesus added that the children of this world are often wiser than the children of God! Jesus went on to explain that he who is faithful in the least is also faithful in much, and he who is unjust in the little is also unjust in much. No servant can serve two masters; he will either hate the one and love the other, or hold to the one and despise the other.

If we read this story on a surface level, it would appear that the steward was still stealing from his master by collecting only a portion of what was owed. Yet, his master commended him because he had discovered the principle of saving for the future. The steward gave his lord's debtors a break and negotiated with them because he was thinking long-term. For us, this story is actually a lesson in money management. We aren't supposed to get into debt and owe large sums of money. Instead, we should save for our futures, demonstrating responsibility. Jesus told this parable to support the truth that money is actually the least important thing in the kingdom of God, and those who can be trusted in financial matters can be trusted in weightier issues.

HINDRANCES TO A GIVING HEART

The biggest hindrance to cultivating a giving heart is the spirit of mammon. Mammon is not money, as some think, but it is actually a demonic spirit that attaches itself to money and seduces people into doing anything to get money. It is the spirit that gets us to hold back on our giving and spend our money on ourselves. It is the spirit that entices people to get money by any means necessary, even if it involves compromise or ungodly behavior. The spirit of mammon is designed to destroy our harvest and keep us in a perpetual cycle of lack and financial ruin. It is essentially the spirit of the world and Christians must be aware of when this spirit is trying to infiltrate their lives.

The spiritual law of seedtime and harvest is supposed to produce results. When it doesn't, we have to examine what may be going on in our lives that is hindering our blessings from manifesting. Often it is our lack of trust in God and our trust in money (inspired by the spirit of mammon) that is the culprit.

We see the story of the rich young ruler in Mark 10:17-30. This story is particularly important for us to understand because it clearly identifies hindrances to freely and generously giving to God. When Jesus had gone forth, the rich young ruler came to him and asked what he needed to do to inherit eternal life. Jesus told him to obey the commandments; the man replied that he had obeyed them since his youth. Jesus then told him that he lacked one thing, and instructed him to sell all that he had, give to the poor, and follow Him. The man couldn't bring himself to do this and went away grieved because he had great possessions.

Jesus' answer to this man was designed to test the man's trust in God and He's asking us to do the same thing today. The part of Jesus' instructions that grieved the man was the giving part. This man saw giving as a loss and not a gain. Because we know that grief is associated with loss, we know that this man valued his possessions more than the opportunity to follow Christ. He turned away the chance to experience true abundance and riches because his heart was wrapped up in his possessions. He was under the influence of the spirit of mammon. Instead of him possessing things, the truth is that his things possessed him.

We don't have to be like the rich young ruler. By committing to value God and trusting Him more than we do our money or possessions, we can prove to ourselves that we are ready for God's blessings to invade our lives. It starts with recognizing that nothing we own really belongs to us; it all belongs to God. When we begin to see our resources as belonging to God, it becomes easier to give because we realize that He is the source of all we have.

Whenever we look at what we have and it is not enough, this is an indication that what we have is actually not our harvest, but rather our seed. We saw this principle when Jesus fed the multitude with five loaves of bread and two fish. He took what looked like "not enough" and multiplied it so that it became more than enough:

> Send them away, that they may go into the country round about, and into the villages, and buy themselves bread: for they have nothing to eat. He answered and said unto them, Give ye them to eat. And they say unto him, Shall we go and buy two hundred pennyworth of bread, and give them to eat? He saith unto them, How many loaves have ye? go and see. And when they knew, they say, Five, and two fishes. And he commanded them to make all sit down by companies upon the green grass. And they sat down in ranks, by hundreds, and by fifties. And when he had taken the five loaves and the two fishes, he looked up to heaven, and blessed, and brake the loaves, and gave them to his disciples to set before them; and the two fishes divided he among them all. And they did all eat, and were filled. And they took up twelve baskets full of the fragments, and of the fishes. And they that did eat of the loaves were about five thousand men (Mark 6:36-44).

Jesus was presented with what appeared to be not enough. Instead of getting into fear, He took what He had, gave thanks for it, blessed it, and broke it. In doing this, the resources multiplied and He was able to feed a multitude of people and have plenty left over. When it appears that you don't have enough, take what you have, thank God for it, and give those resources where God instructs. This is how you "break bread." When you do this in faith, you can have confidence that God will multiply what you have and provide for your need.

Faith in what God says about finances and demonstrating your trust in Him through giving are the keys to an abundant life. It actually makes more of a difference than anything else on which we could depend. God cannot lie. If He tells us to give, then we can rest assured that there is a blessing attached to that instruction. When we trust God with our finances and refuse to allow the spirit of mammon to dictate what we do with our money, we prove our readiness to receive more of what God has for us.

Study Questions

1. True or False: Your giving demonstrates whether you trust God.

2. Why should every Christian be a giver? _____
   _____
   _____

3. Why do we give? _____
   _____

4. How should we give? _____

5. To whom should we give? _____
   _____

6. True or False: Money is bad.

7. What does God want us to see about ourselves through our giving?
   _____

8. True or False: Money is the least of all things in the kingdom of God.

9. Why did the rich young ruler go away grieved at Jesus's answer to him?
   _____

10. What are the keys to the abundant life? _____
    _____
    _____

SCRIPTURE REFERENCES

Luke 16:1-13

Mark 10:17-30

Mark 6:36-44

Haggai 1:6, 7

Luke 9:13-17

Numbers 23:19

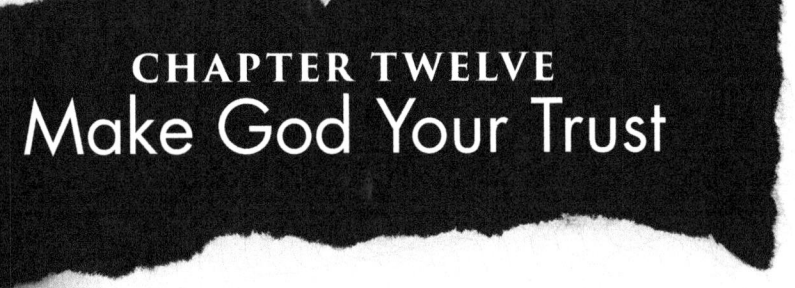

CHAPTER TWELVE
Make God Your Trust

When you walk into a room and flip the light switch, do you wonder whether or not the light is going to come on? Or, when you go to sit down in a chair, do you fear that the chair will collapse under your weight? The answer to both of these questions is no. We typically have complete faith and trust that when we turn the light switch on, we will see light, and when we sit down in a chair, we will be supported. Well, when it comes to the kingdom of God and receiving what Jesus has made available to you under the new covenant, trusting God is vital. In fact, trust is the currency of God's kingdom. In the Bible, we see wonderful examples of people who trusted God completely, but there are also people who demonstrated that they had more trust in their material possessions than they did in God. The rich young ruler was one of these examples. He was under the influence of the spirit of mammon. Money is a key topic in the Word of God and the message that God wants us to receive is that we are not to put our trust in money but put our trust in Him alone.

There are those who feel that money is an off-limits topic in the Christian community, but nothing is further from the truth. The Scriptures talk about money so often that it is impossible to avoid studying God's heart on the matter. The issue is trust. Everything in the kingdom of God is based on faith and trust, and we must learn to trust God with the financial realm. The spirit of mammon is the spirit of the world. It is designed to get us to put our trust in money and self-effort more than we do God. When we get away from trusting in Him, money becomes our god by default. When this happens, we open ourselves up to every foul influence and suggestion of the devil to get us to compromise and do anything necessary to obtain money. God will not force us to trust in Him; the decision is completely ours to make.

BENEFITS OF TRUSTING GOD

To trust in someone is to rely on, lean on, and have confidence in them. Jesus tells us to rely on Him and not on mammon. This can be a challenge in today's culture and society, which is driven by the desire to obtain money by any means necessary, even at the expense of your soul. Even still, trusting God is the way to go and has multiple benefits.

Jesus taught on the topic of trust and the financial realm on many occasions. The things He said often caused dismay in His followers. For example, in Mark 10:24, He said that it was extremely difficult for those who trust in riches to enter into the kingdom of God. While Jesus referenced money in His lesson here, the underlying issue He was addressing with His disciples was trust. He knows the human tendency to put trust in money, so He was letting us know that doing so will cause great damage to our lives. We must put our trust in God, not our money.

The ultimate indicator of trusting God is your ability to give. Jesus observed people putting money in the treasury and He commended one particular woman who gave the little that she had (Mark 12:41-44). She caught His attention even more than those who were giving large amounts because her gift was coming from a place of true trust. It was all she had and she gave her last. God looks at the condition of our hearts as it relates to our finances. These are the money tests that demonstrate to Him where our true confidence lies.

The book of Proverbs has familiar passages of Scripture that show us the power in trusting God rather than ourselves or anything outside of ourselves. *"Trust in the LORD with all thine heart; and lean not unto thine own understanding. In all thy ways acknowledge him, and he shall direct thy paths. Be not wise in thine own eyes: fear the LORD, and depart from evil. It shall be health to thy navel, and marrow to thy bones. Honour the LORD with thy substance, and with the firstfruits of all thine increase: So shall thy barns be filled with plenty, and thy presses shall burst out with new wine"* (Proverbs 3:5-10).

When we trust in God with all our heart and don't lean to our own understanding, He promises to guide us in what we do. The Scripture shows us that trusting God at this level even has physical benefits and causes us to be in good health. Acknowledging Him before doing anything ensures that we include Him in our plans and position ourselves for the best outcome. He promises to direct and increase us so that our bank accounts are overflowing with provision. We are to trust God and honor *Him* with our money, rather than trusting in our money.

The book of Isaiah gives us some more amazing promises that come with trusting God. For example, it says that when we keep our minds focused on Jesus, we will be kept in perfect peace (Isaiah 26:3-5). The reason we are kept in perfect peace is because we trust in Him. Any time our peace is disrupted, we must remember that it is an indication that we have gotten our focus off of Jesus and on our circumstances. When this happens, we are going to be tempted to trust in money or our own ability to get money, which lets us know the spirit of mammon is at work. The key is to refocus our attention on the Word of God so that we can continue to lean and rely on Him as our source. An unwavering trust in God ushers His provision into our lives.

The book of Psalms has many other powerful passages that reinforce the benefit of trusting God alone. *"But I trusted in thee, O LORD: I said, Thou art my God. My times are in thy hand: deliver me from the hand of mine enemies, and from them that persecute me. Make thy face to shine upon thy servant: save me for thy mercies' sake"* (Psalm 31:14-16). The psalmist refers to God's grace and asks to be saved, not because he deserves it, but because of God's mercy. God simply needs our faith and trust. When we trust in Him, we access His deliverance and protection in every situation and circumstance that we face.

OUR DECISION

"Blessed is that man that maketh the LORD his trust, and respecteth not the proud, nor such as turn aside to lies" (Psalm 40:4). God is not going to force us to trust Him; we have to choose to do so as an act of our will. We have to decide to either trust in our ability or trust God to take care of us. You see, when you decide to trust God, you are empowered to prosper. Hebrews 4:11 says, *"Let us labour therefore to enter into that rest, lest any man fall after the same example of unbelief."* Resting in the finished works of Jesus is another way to demonstrate our trust in God. The picture of trust is in our refusal to carry worries, cares, or anxiety about anything concerning our lives. When we get to this place of rest, we are truly trusting God and we are allowing Him to provide for us.

The spirit of mammon is designed to get our focus off of God and on ourselves and our possessions. It is the spirit of the world and it wants to thrust us into a cycle of self-effort, compromise, and obsession with obtaining money at any cost. The Word of God tells us that we cannot serve two masters; we cannot serve God and the spirit of mammon

(Luke 16:13). God is calling every believer to make a choice. Just like in the Old Testament, He tells us to choose whom we will serve (Joshua 24:15). This is a choice that we will have to make every day of our lives.

Since the beginning of time, man has tried to do things without involving God. The results have always fallen short because God did not create us to live independent of Him and His assistance. When we try to do things in our own ability, we will always fail, no matter how much progress we appear to make. We see this clearly in the book of Genesis, when the people decided that they were going to build a city and tower that reached heaven. They got into pride and self-effort, and God humbled them (Genesis 11:4). The mindset of these people is really where the "self-help" philosophy came from. It is a mentality that says we can improve ourselves by ourselves. It seeks to make the individual their own god and leave God out of the equation. Inspiration with God and without the Word of God is a deceptive trap that will only lead to trouble. When we declare we don't need God, either in word or deed, self-effort and the Law of Moses take over; and the door to the spirit of mammon is opened. On the other hand, the covenant between God and Abraham was a grace covenant. Abraham didn't *do* anything to receive favor from God since there was no law before Moses presented it. God lets us see through the life of Abraham that pure, unadulterated trust in Him alone for favor, ability, and righteousness is the key to a thriving life. Nothing we can do in and of ourselves can sustain itself.

THE BEAUTY OF THE COVENANT OF GRACE

The covenant of grace was sealed by the blood of Jesus after His death and resurrection, but the grace of God was in operation even in the Old Testament. Mankind was actually under grace until the people chose to live by the Law of Moses. Before Moses brought the commandments of God to the people and they said, "*...All that the Lord hath spoken we will do*" (Exodus 19:8), God had a covenant with Abraham based on His grace, not Abraham's ability to keep laws and commandments. The Law of Moses and its consequences were activated when the people decided to try and live according to their own ability versus trusting God. They decided that they were going to make, or produce, results by their own efforts. Their confidence was in themselves, not God.

The Ten Commandments were actually the people's introduction to the Law of Moses. In those sets of laws they were commanded to worship God only and not have any other gods. Not surprisingly, as soon as the laws were given, the people made a golden calf. Even though God was angry with the people, He still showed grace when Moses interceded for them and reminded Him of the previous Abrahamic covenant. God actually wanted to wipe mankind off the face of the earth. This was a consequence of sin under the law.

The beauty of the covenant of grace that Abraham experienced, and that we now have access to through the blood of Jesus, is that we all receive the same reward, but we do not reap a curse when we sin or miss the mark like people did under the law. Under this covenant, God still blesses us when we make a mistake. We will not be judged and condemned for our actions because, in Christ, our sins and mistakes are not charged to our accounts (Romans 4:8).

> For the kingdom of heaven is like unto a man that is an householder, which went out early in the morning to hire labourers into his vineyard. And when he had agreed with the labourers for a penny a day, he sent them into his vineyard. And he went out about the third hour, and saw others standing idle in the marketplace, And said unto them; Go ye also into the vineyard, and whatsoever is right I will give you. And they went

their way. Again he went out about the sixth and ninth hour, and did likewise. And about the eleventh hour he went out, and found others standing idle, and saith unto them, Why stand ye here all the day idle? They say unto him, Because no man hath hired us. He saith unto them, Go ye also into the vineyard; and whatsoever is right, that shall ye receive. So when even was come, the lord of the vineyard saith unto his steward, Call the labourers, and give them their hire, beginning from the last unto the first. And when they came that were hired about the eleventh hour, they received every man a penny. But when the first came, they supposed that they should have received more; and they likewise received every man a penny. And when they had received it, they murmured against the goodman of the house, Saying, These last have wrought but one hour, and thou hast made them equal unto us, which have borne the burden and heat of the day. But he answered one of them, and said, Friend, I do thee no wrong: didst not thou agree with me for a penny? Take that thine is, and go thy way: I will give unto this last, even as unto thee. Is it not lawful for me to do what I will with mine own? Is thine eye evil, because I am good? So the last shall be first, and the first last: for many be called, but few chosen (Matthew 20:1-16).

The message in this powerful parable is this: no matter how long a believer has been saved, every Christian will receive the same grace from God. This is the beauty of the covenant of grace. God's favor does not take into consideration how long we have been doing something. It is not based on what we have or haven't done. It is based on what we believe and our trust in Him. It is impossible to live this Christian life without God. In Him we live, move, and have our very being (Acts

17:28). We were not created to journey through this life on our own, but were designed to carry God with us everywhere we go and in everything we do. Even Jesus admitted that He did nothing apart from the Father (John 5:19).

We must come to a place where we admit we need God and submit to Him in every area of our lives. We were created to live in close relationship with Him, leaning on, relying on, and trusting in Him. When we trust God, we set ourselves up for continual provision, blessings, and increase. Our ability, money, or resources cannot sustain us, but God can and He desires to be an integral part of our lives. Trust Him with everything that concerns you and experience the joy that comes from living in total reliance on Him for all your needs and desires.

Study Questions

1. _____ is a key topic in the Bible.

2. What does God want to teach us as it relates to money? _____
   _____

3. When we get away from trusting God, money becomes our _____
   _____ by default.

4. What does it mean to trust God? _____

5. What is the human tendency when it comes to money? _____
   _____

6. What is the ultimate indicator that you trust God with your money?
   _____

7. Why did Jesus commend the woman who gave a small amount of money? _____

8. What is the self-help mentality about? _____
   _____

9. What is the spirit of mammon designed to do? _____
   _____

10. What is the beauty of the covenant of grace? _____
    _____
    _____

SCRIPTURE REFERENCES

Mark 10:24

Mark 12:41-44

Proverbs 3:5-10

Isaiah 26:3-5

Psalm 31:14-16

Psalm 40:4

Hebrews 4:11

Luke 16:13

Joshua 24:15

Genesis 11:4

Exodus 19:7-12

Romans 4:8

Matthew 20:1-16

Acts 17:28

John 5:19

CHAPTER THIRTEEN
The Money-Trust Connection: God vs. Mammon

There is one topic that is guaranteed to get people talking and it is money. Money management and issues pertaining to the financial realm tend to sharply divide those in the body of Christ. Many believers do not believe that finances have any place in spiritual conversations but, when we study the Word of God, we see that this is simply not the case. The Scriptures teach that money is least in the kingdom of God and actually requires the smallest amount of faith. By contrast, most Christians have been taught the exact opposite. Now, the tendency is to think that money is actually the most important thing in our lives. Thinking of money this way affects our emotions, robs us of our peace, and causes us to panic. Studying the Scriptures teaches us the correct way of thinking about wealth, and we learn to trust God with our finances. When we demonstrate that we trust God with our money, we can trust Him for bigger things as well.

One of the most significant ways that we can demonstrate our trust in God is by proving our faithfulness in money matters. Throughout His ministry, Jesus taught parables related to trusting God in the financial arena and how important it is in our lives:

And he said also unto his disciples, There was a certain rich man, which had a steward; and the same was accused unto him that he had wasted his goods. And he called him, and said unto him, How is it that I hear this of thee? give an account of thy stewardship; for thou mayest be no longer steward. Then the steward said within himself, What shall I do? for my lord taketh away from me the stewardship: I cannot dig; to beg I am ashamed. I am resolved what to do, that, when I am put out of the stewardship, they may receive me into their houses. So he called every one of his lord's debtors unto him, and said unto the first, How much owest thou unto my lord? And he said, An hundred measures of oil. And he said unto him, Take thy bill, and sit down quickly, and write fifty. Then said he to another, And how much owest thou? And he said, An hundred measures of wheat. And he said unto him, Take thy bill, and write fourscore. And the lord commended the unjust steward, because he had done wisely: for the children of this world are in their generation wiser than the children of light. And I say unto you, Make to yourselves friends of the mammon of unrighteousness; that, when ye fail, they may receive you into everlasting habitations. He that is faithful in that which is least is faithful also in much: and he that is unjust in the least is unjust also in the much. If therefore ye have not been faithful in the unrighteous mammon, who will commit to your trust the true riches? And if ye have not been faithful in that which is another man's, who shall give you that which is your own? No servant can serve two masters: for either he will hate the one, and love the other; or else he will hold to the one, and despise the other. Ye cannot serve God and mammon (Luke 16:1-13).

This parable provides us with a great opportunity to learn about money management as sons of God. Jesus told His disciples this story about the steward who was dismissed from his position for wasting his master's goods. When the steward went to each of his master's debtors and told them to pay only a portion of what they owed, his master commended him for doing wisely. Jesus emphasized that he who is faithful in that which is least is also faithful in much, and he who is unjust in the least is also unjust in much. The wisdom that the master saw was that the steward was planning for his future. When we bless others with our money, our actions have eternal impact. Being faithful, in this context, means being trustworthy and making a continuous commitment to do the right thing with our finances. This highlights the question of whether we can be trusted to act with integrity with our finances, which is the least of the areas requiring faith. We must master the financial realm according to *God's* way of doing things.

The biblical concept of sowing and reaping contradicts what the spirit of mammon says. This spirit tells us to hoard our money and keep it to ourselves. The truth is that giving isn't really about the money but it is about the condition of our hearts. When we walk in the confidence of Jesus, our trust in God will grow. We must examine how healthy our trust is in this financial arena and refuse to cast away our confidence because it has a great recompense of reward (Hebrews 10:35). When we are faithful to give what God says give, when He says give, and to whom He says to give, our faith will be rewarded. We simply must have patience and wait until we see results.

Jesus is deeply interested in people's relationship with money. Trust is the currency of God's kingdom. John 16:33 says, *"These things I have spoken unto you, that in me ye might have peace. In the world ye shall have tribulation: but be of good cheer; I have overcome the world."* While this level of trust can be challenging to maintain when things get tough and we go through tribulations, it is the type of trust that puts it all on the line and completely relies on God's provision.

When the rich young ruler asked Jesus how to inherit eternal life, Jesus told him to sell everything he had, give to the poor, and follow Him. The young man went away grieved, and Jesus told His disciples that it is extremely difficult for those who trust in riches to enter the kingdom of God (Mark 10:17-30). The rich young ruler was operating under the Law of Moses when he said he had kept the law since his youth. It is impossible to keep every single commandment; therefore, he lied when he said he did. He was deceived into thinking he had done so because it is an impossible feat. He trusted in his wealth more than he trusted in God. As a result, he forfeited the opportunity to follow Jesus and reap the benefits of a personal relationship with Him. What Jesus was asking of him required him to be faithful with the least—money—but he couldn't bring himself to do so. We have to make sure that we are not found lacking in the area of trust when God calls on us to give of our material possessions.

Remember that Satan does *not* want you to give your money into the kingdom of God and he will never tell you to do so. In fact, he is the spirit behind the times you "choke" when it is time to give. He will make you feel as if you need to hold on to your money instead of giving it to another person, ministry, or pastor. He knows that when you pass the money test, you prove to yourself that your trust is in God alone. When you know you trust God with the least, you will have the faith and confidence to trust God for greater manifestations of the supernatural.

God is opposed to the spirit of mammon and vice versa. As Christians, we can overcome this spirit by purposing in our hearts to give liberally and regularly as soon as we feel prompted to do so. When we feel like we don't want to give our money, that is precisely the time that we need to do so. In fact, we can challenge ourselves to defeat the spirit of mammon by making a quality decision to give as much as possible, at every opportunity, and from a cheerful heart. This is how you will pass the trust-test and make the money-trust connection for maximum results in every area of your life.

Study Questions

1. What issue tends to sharply divide the body of Christ the most?
   _____

2. What is one of the most significant ways we demonstrate our trust in God? _____

3. He who is faithful in the _____ is also faithful in the _____.

4. What does the parable of the unjust steward teach us? _____
   _____

5. True or False: The concept of sowing and reaping contradicts what the spirit of mammon says.

6. True or False: Jesus is deeply interested in people's relationship with money.

7. Why did the rich young ruler forfeit an opportunity to follow Jesus?
   _____
   _____

8. True or False: When you are hesitant to give financially, the spirit of mammon is at work.

9. When you pass the money test, what do you prove? _____
   _____

10. How can believers overcome the spirit of mammon? _____

_____

SCRIPTURE REFERENCES

Luke 16:1-13

Hebrews 10:35

Mark 12:41-44

John 16:33

Mark 10:17-30

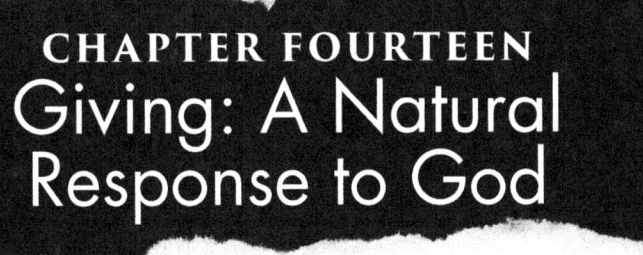

CHAPTER FOURTEEN
Giving: A Natural Response to God

There is a way that we are to live as believers that should be just as natural as eating, sleeping, and breathing. For the Christian, giving isn't something we do out of obligation, it is actually supposed to be a natural reflex that is born out of true love and appreciation for God. He wants us to know how to properly handle our financial resources and not even think twice about our giving. The apostle Paul had a lot to say about grace-based giving, and what he preached is unlike the advice that you typically hear in the world today. His emphasis was on giving generously as a way to demonstrate trust for God and also activate the spiritual principles needed for your increase. For grace-based giving to work in our lives, we must avoid the trap of giving too little and expecting too much. The issue here is actually not about money at all, but about how much we love and trust God. Some people are afraid to part with their finances; but when we think about what Jesus has done in our lives and how He has delivered us from bad situations time and time again, giving becomes an automatic response. Opening our hands and letting the money flow freely will result in blessings for everyone involved.

One of the things Paul taught about giving was that believers are to give joyfully and abundantly. Giving demonstrates our trust in God and is a reflection of our awareness of God's grace in our lives. In fact, grace is what enables us to give freely.

Galatians 1:8, 9 discusses the Gospel of Grace being the only true gospel: *"But though we, or an angel from heaven, preach any other gospel unto you than that which we have preached unto you, let him be accursed. As we said before, so say I now again, if any man preach any other gospel unto you than that ye have received, let him be accursed."* When Paul explained that the gospel is the good news of the grace of Christ, he repeated himself on this point for clarity and emphasis. If Paul is the standard by which the preaching of grace is to be measured and judged, then we must examine what he taught on finances, prosperity, and giving.

Second Corinthians 9:6 is a foundational Scripture that shows us the importance of having a generous heart when giving: *"But this I say, He which soweth sparingly shall reap also sparingly; and he which soweth bountifully shall reap also bountifully."* The Greek translation of "sparingly" is "stingy." Paul taught proportional giving when he addressed finances. This means that what we give should be in proportion to what God has given us. For example, if we have been blessed with much, we should make it our business to give much. No matter what season we are in financially, we are all able to give generously and in proportion to what we have. God will never ask us to give more than what He has blessed us to give. We only need to give according to the grace that is on our lives.

Another important point to consider is that God does not measure our financial gifts in monetary amounts, but in percentage and in our attitude toward giving. For example, for the person who has $10,000 in the bank, a $1,000 offering is a small percentage to give; but for the person who has $50 in the bank, $35 would be a large offering. The heart-attitude of demonstrating trust in God to the point of giving almost all you have from a place of cheerfulness and joy is what God is looking for. He wants to see if you really believe His Word on finances.

God cannot be mocked; whatever a man sows is what he reaps (Galatians 6:7). As it relates to finances, this means that whatever goes out of your hands determines what comes back to you. Many people struggle with this concept, but our giving truly is an example of our trust in God. *"Give, and it shall be given unto you; good measure, pressed down, and shaken together, and running over, shall men give into your bosom. For with the same measure that ye mete withal it shall be measured to you again"* (Luke 6:38). The law of seedtime and harvest never stops. What we give we will also receive. As believers, we can't dismiss the truth of this principle. We should not expect to receive an abundant harvest if we have not given abundantly! It just doesn't work that way.

BLESSINGS FOR THE GIVER

Did you know that giving doesn't just bless the receiver, but it also blesses the giver? There are four very specific things that will happen as a result of our decision to trust God with our resources:

1. We demonstrate the sincerity and proof of our love for God. Giving is a love-motivated action. In every relationship, including our relationship with God, it is a reflex of love.
2. When we give, we receive a blessing. This blessing isn't a physical reward (although we can expect to receive that too), but it is an empowerment that allows us to do things that go beyond our natural abilities.
3. Others' needs are met and we can be a blessing to someone else, which is a wonderful feeling.

4. Giving results in thanksgiving and praise unto God. Our giving can actually prevent misfortune in someone else's life, which causes others to praise God.

We can begin to train ourselves to give by making a habit of setting money aside at the top of the week. Paul reminded us of this: *"Upon the first day of the week let every one of you lay by him in store, as God hath prospered him, that there be no gatherings when I come"* (1 Corinthians 16:2). Paul was reminding the church to put God first in their finances. He didn't want to have to take up an offering when he arrived. This is a powerful way to begin cultivating the mindset of making God a priority in the financial arena of your life.

There will always be trials that come to try to steal our joy and faith in God, but we must refuse to be overtaken by these things. Circumstances will often arise that challenge our decision to give no matter what, but we have to remain steadfast in the face of adversity. Joy is a choice we make regardless of our financial situations. Second Corinthians 8:2 says, *"How that in a great trial of affliction the abundance of their joy and their deep poverty abounded unto the riches of their liberality."* Anything we are facing that challenges our decision to give can be overcome by the grace of God. It is during the times that we are most challenged that we actually find the supernatural ability to push through the fear and give to God anyway, which results in a tremendous blessing being released in our lives. *"For our light affliction, which is but for a moment, worketh for us a far more exceeding and eternal weight of glory"* (2 Corinthians 4:17).

Rest assured that if you are giving from the heart, God will provide you with seed to sow. This is promised in the Word of God (2 Corinthians 9:10). God ministers seed to those who have purposed in their hearts to give, and He multiplies your seed. If you don't have seed, ask yourself if you are truly a giver. The more you develop into one who sows from a heart of love and genuine desire to impact people's lives and expand the kingdom of God, the more you will find resources to sow coming into your hands. We can learn from Paul's teachings on how to grow in grace-based giving as a natural response, so that we can begin to experience all that God has for us.

Study Questions

1. Giving should be a _____ for the believer.

2. Why did Paul emphasize generous giving? _____
   _____
   _____

3. What trap must Christians avoid for grace-based giving to work in our lives? _____

4. How are Christians to give? _____

5. What does giving demonstrate? _____
   _____

6. What does "sparingly" mean? _____

7. What is proportional giving? _____
   _____

8. How does God measure our financial gifts? _____
   _____

9. True or False: The amount you give determines the amount of your harvest.

10. True or False: If you don't have seed to sow you are not a giver.

SCRIPTURE REFERENCES

Galatians 1:8, 9

2 Corinthians 9:2, 6, 10, 12

1 Corinthians 16:2

Galatians 6:7

2 Corinthians 8:2, 8, 14, 24

2 Corinthians 4:17

Luke 6:38

Mark 12:41-44

John 3:16

Acts 20:35

CHAPTER FIFTEEN
Principles of Giving

Principles of Giving

By exploring the truths Paul taught about giving under the new covenant, we can gain an understanding of how we are to flow in grace-based giving as believers. Giving shouldn't be something we do under compulsion or obligation, but as a natural reflex and a part of our character. Paul preached strongly in this area and encouraged Christians to give with the right motives. He taught that giving blesses both the giver and the receiver. There is a harvest that comes with proper giving. Money that comes into a Christian's life should take on the form of either bread to be consumed or seed to be sown. There is no multiplication to be had when we consume our money on bread, but there is multiplication on the seed that we sow. Giving is one of the primary purposes for which we work at our jobs. Our attitude and heart-motivations concerning our giving are important. Our generous giving into matters affecting others will create rejoicing and thanksgiving to God by those who are blessed by us. When we apply these principles, we will have a powerful impact not only on our lives but on others as well.

The primary motive for our giving should be a desire to help others. The truth is that we honor God when we give. We determine the measure of our return by the amount we give (2 Corinthians 9:6). We have the authority in this area to control how much, or how little, we reap, which is powerful. Some Christians do not sow anything anymore, but we should not be able to see someone in need and not be moved to do what we can to help them.

Paul also taught about purposeful giving, as evidenced by his instructions to the church at Corinth: "*Upon the first day of the week let every one of you lay by him in store, as God hath prospered him, that there be no gatherings when I come*"(1 Corinthians 16:2). This Scripture focuses on giving with a purpose and setting your mind to do so in advance. Giving is a way to honor God and is extremely pleasing in His sight. When we honor someone or something, we are assigning value to that person or thing. When we give and make giving to Him first our priority, we are demonstrating our honor for Him and choosing to put Him first in our lives.

Giving is an act of faith and love, and should never be done out of fear. Like Paul taught, we should give on purpose. In Mark 12:41-44, we see Jesus observing people put money into the treasury. At one point, a poor widow woman came and threw in two mites. Her act of giving a seemingly small amount got Jesus' attention to the point that He used it as an opportunity to teach His disciples an important lesson about giving. Even though people were putting large amounts of money in the treasury, this woman's gift was more valuable because it was pretty much all she had.

Giving is still very important to Jesus because our money is what we have a tendency to trust. This is why there are so many scriptural instructions about financial giving. God knows it is an area in which we tend to get off track, so He constantly challenges us to recalibrate our priorities by getting us out of our comfort zones where our money is concerned. He wants us to give back to Him what the world trusts, which is why tithes and offerings are so important. Money is the currency of exchange in the world, but trust is the currency of exchange in the kingdom of God.

Second Corinthians 9:10 says, "*Now he that ministereth seed to the sower both minister bread for your food, and multiply your seed sown, and increase the fruits of your righteousness.*" Paul explained that money should take two forms: as bread to meet our needs, and as seed to sow toward helping others. If we consume too much of our bread and do not sow enough seed, we run into issues in the physical realm. It is up to us to avoid hyper-consumption and not spend one hundred percent of our seed. If we tend to spend all our money and have nothing left to sow, we need to make some adjustments and renew our minds in order to get our priorities back in place. Similarly, we should give because we have purposed in our hearts to do so, not as an afterthought. It is good to get in the habit of believing in the multiplication of what we give. As we study the concept of sowing, our faith will grow in this area. Faith comes by hearing and hearing by the Word of God (Romans 10:17), so the more we hear the truth about God's system of giving, the more our faith to give will grow.

Grace-based giving is all about relying on *God* to meet our needs, not our own efforts or labor. When we get into the flow of giving the way God intended, we will begin to see that our jobs are not our source. Our employment is there to support our desire to give into the lives of other people. In this context, we live by our giving. We have to transition to this way of thinking in order to truly live according to kingdom principles on the earth.

GIVE BECAUSE YOU WANT TO

It is one thing to give out of obligation, but it is another thing to give because you want to. Willful giving is pleasing to God and generous sowing guarantees a generous harvest. Paul emphasizes this when he says that everyone should give what they have purposed in their hearts to give, not grudgingly or of necessity, because God loves a cheerful giver (2 Corinthians 9:7). Our attitude toward giving and our motivations behind it really do matter. Under the Law of Moses, the people tithed out of necessity in order to be blessed. Under the new covenant, however, we give out of gratitude, thanksgiving, and love for God.

Grace-based giving was in operation even before the law was instituted. Abraham, the father of faith, experienced favor in battle when God delivered his enemies into his hand. As a result of God's goodness, Abraham was moved to give a tithe of all the spoils of victory to the high priest (Genesis 14:14-24). This is the blueprint for how God wants us to operate in our giving. It is to be an immediate reflex to God blessing us. The world tries to get us into fear when it comes to giving, fear of being taken advantage of and fear of running out; but we can believe God in our finances. The blessing of the Lord makes rich and adds no sorrow to our lives (Proverbs 10:22).

Giving financially is the number one way to prove to ourselves that we trust God. It enables us to determine our own harvest. *"But this I say, He which soweth sparingly shall reap also sparingly; and he which soweth bountifully shall reap also bountifully. Every man according as he purposeth in his heart, so let him give; not grudgingly, or of necessity: for God loveth a cheerful giver. And God is able to make all grace abound toward you; that ye, always having all sufficiency in all things, may abound to every good work"* (2 Corinthians 9:6-8). For those who doubt the guarantee that if we sow, we will get something back, this promise is biblical proof that we will. God will cause our lives to be enriched in every area, which will ultimately cause thanksgiving to Him

(2 Corinthians 9:11). This principle is so powerful that, when we put it into practice, it can even cause unbelievers to experience God and give thanks to Him.

Financial blessings in our lives give us the opportunity to be a blessing to others. When we become funnels through which God can flow His favor into the lives of others, then we become blessings. This was what He intended before the foundation of the world. When we take care of others' needs through our financial resources, we actually become God's hands in the earth. It is the reason He puts us in a position to have resources in the first place. By becoming proficient in giving and obeying God with our material possessions, we demonstrate the character of Jesus and set ourselves up for increase, promotion, and an abundance of favor.

Study Questions

1. True or False: Giving is a part of Christian character.

2. Giving blesses both the _____ and the _____.

3. What are the two forms money should take in a believer's life? _____

4. What is a result of generously giving into the lives of others? _____

5. What should be the primary motive for our giving? _____

6. True or False: We can determine the amount of our harvest.

7. What does it mean to honor something? _____

8. What is purposeful giving? _____

9. True or False: Grace-based giving was in operation before the Law of Moses was established.

10. True or False: We always get something back when we give.

SCRIPTURE REFERENCES

2 Corinthians 9:6-8, 10, 11

1 Corinthians 16:2

Mark 12:41-44

Romans 10:17

Genesis 14:14-24

Proverbs 10:22

Galatians 1:8, 9

2 Corinthians 8:2

Ephesians 4:28

Acts 20:33-35

Luke 16:13

Philippians 4:10

CHAPTER SIXTEEN
Giving: A Christian Priority

A lifestyle of giving is integral to a believer and is a key component of how God expects us to live. Throughout the New Testament, Paul writes about giving and what the heart behind it should be. Paul's teachings are significant when compared to other biblical writers because he was entrusted with the direct revelation of the Gospel of Grace. He was the *apostle* of grace. The financial realm is one of the areas in which many Christians have not had significant success. It's one of those areas that many believers have not been able to conquer, but God wants us to master the financial arena. Money is a major issue in the lives of so many people and the thing that the largest percentage of our lives is centered around. Paul's teachings give us hope that we can have success in the financial arena and the Word of God helps us to build our faith. God's love is all-encompassing, which means that we can come to Him for help in any area in which we need it, including finances. However, we must believe and trust in God.

Money is probably one of the most widely misunderstood topics in the Bible because there are so many misconceptions about what God really thinks and feels about us having it. Contrary to what religion may have taught us, God is concerned with our financial condition. He is also concerned with the condition of our hearts as it relates to finances. Jesus cares deeply about money and how it affects us. It is simply wrong to assume that God has nothing to do with it or that He *wants* nothing to do with it. We must believe what the Scriptures say about money because God's promises to us will not work or come to pass if we don't believe them. Tradition makes the Word of God of no effect (Mark 7:13).

Studying Paul's teachings is critical because Paul was the apostle of grace. He was appointed to this office by Jesus Christ, Himself. Galatians 1:1-9 gives us a clear understanding of who Paul was and why he was qualified to teach us God's heart on matters that pertain to the believer:

> Paul, an apostle, (not of men, neither by man, but by Jesus Christ, and God the Father, who raised him from the dead;) And all the brethren which are with me, unto the churches of Galatia: Grace be to you and peace from God the Father, and from our Lord Jesus Christ, Who gave himself for our sins, that he might deliver us from this present evil world, according to the will of God and our Father: To whom be glory for ever and ever. Amen. I marvel that ye are so soon removed from him that called you into the grace of Christ unto another gospel: Which is not another; but there be some that trouble you, and would pervert the gospel of Christ. But though we, or an angel from heaven, preach any other gospel unto you than that which we have preached unto you, let him be accursed. As we said before, so say I now again, if any man preach any other gospel unto you than that ye have received, let him be accursed.

This passage of Scripture lets us know several things. First, Paul was not called or appointed to the office of apostle by man, but by God, Himself. Also, there is no such thing as a "prosperity gospel," as many critics believe. The only real gospel is the Gospel of Christ, also known as the Gospel of Grace. This is the only gospel that Paul acknowledges. He actually says that there are those who pervert this message, trying to turn it into something that it is not. The Gospel of Grace is the message of God's unmerited, undeserved favor toward us; this favor is available for every area of our lives, including our finances. If someone preaches a "gospel" and it doesn't line up with what Paul preaches, it is not truly *the* gospel.

GIVING IS A HEART ISSUE

As it relates to finances, Paul had a lot to say. Giving is based on the principle of seedtime and harvest, as evidenced by Second Corinthians 9:6, which says that he who sows sparingly will reap sparingly, but he who sows bountifully will reap bountifully. Our giving and the return that we receive from our giving is in proportion to the blessings that God has bestowed on us. He wants us to give from a generous heart, and not with a grudging attitude. This is what God is concerned about the most when it comes to giving our substance and resources. He gave us the authority to determine how much of a harvest we receive. This is the same authority Jesus gave the disciples when He told them to heal the sick, cast out demons, and raise the dead (Matthew 10:1, 8).

First Corinthians 16:2 gives us a picture of what giving as a priority looks like. In this passage of Scripture, Paul instructs the church to set aside the offerings in advance: *"Upon the first day of the week let every one of you lay by him in store, as God hath prospered him, that there be no gatherings when I come."* Paul was communicating the importance of not making giving an afterthought. God uses our giving as a tool to keep us from being self-centered, which is so easy to do. The system that God has set up is not only designed to bring increase into our hands but to develop our character and help us to become more Christ-like.

Having a heart that is liberal when it comes to giving also increases our joy and vice versa. *"The liberal soul shall be made fat: and he that watereth shall be watered also himself"* (Proverbs 11:25). Giving brings joy to the heart of the giver! In Second Corinthians 8:2, Paul commended the Macedonian church for having great joy in spite of their financial condition, and noted how what appeared to be financial lack put them in a position to develop the joy of the Lord and give even more. Giving truly is the way to experience great blessings from God.

Christians are supposed to be givers. Our willingness to give indicates our level of trust in God. In fact, the money issue has always been, and always will be, about trusting God. In the book of Mark, we see Jesus sitting against the treasury, watching people put money into it (Mark 12:41-44). There were rich people who were giving a lot of money, but what really caught Jesus' attention was a poor widow who came and threw in two mites, which equal about a farthing. He called His disciples to Him and let them know that this woman put more in the treasury than all of the people who sowed out of their abundance. She sowed all that she had, which equated to a greater level of giving than those whose offerings barely made a dent in their financial earnings. These are the things God is looking at when we give. Do we trust God with *all* that we have? Do we only give when it is convenient or within our budgets? Are we giving small amounts in comparison to the much that is in our bank accounts? Are we willing to give it all if God instructs us to do so? Every time Jesus talked about money, it was really an issue of trust.

The story of the rich young ruler is another one that we can study to understand God's heart on the issue of giving. This young man approached Jesus and asked Him what he needed to do to inherit eternal life. Jesus told him to obey the commandments (remember He was still operating under the Law of Moses), and the man answered that he had obeyed all of them since childhood. Jesus told him to sell all that he had, give it to the poor, and take up his cross and follow Him. When the man heard what was required of him, he turned away and left. His heart was wrapped up in his possessions and he couldn't bring himself to part with them (Mark 10:17-24). Jesus' answer to the man's question involved money and possessions, and it was designed to test his trust in God.

If we want to be givers, God knows how to get seed into our hands. Second Corinthians 9:10 says, *"Now he that ministereth seed to the sower both minister bread for your food, and multiply your seed sown, and increase the fruits of your righteousness."* This is a promise. The multiplication that will come is on the seed we give, not on the bread we consume for ourselves. *"Let him who stole steal no more, but rather let him labor, working with his hands the thing which is good, that he may have to give to him who needs"* (Ephesians 4:28). We work so that we can help others. Our employment or method of financial increase is designed to provide us with seed we can sow into others' lives.

Giving and supporting the needs of others is the responsibility of every Christian, and it starts in the church, among leadership. Paul says, *"I have coveted no man's silver, gold, or apparel. You yourselves know that these hands have ministered to my necessities, and to them who were with me. I have showed you all things, how that so laboring you ought to support the weak, and to remember the words of our Lord Jesus, how he said it is more blessed to give than to receive"* (Acts 20:33-35). He was teaching that church leadership must demonstrate the giving principle by example. When this happens, the spirit of giving that God intended from the beginning will translate to those in the body of Christ.

Giving is not a burden but a privilege and an honor from God. When we give of our substance, we demonstrate we trust God with our resources, time, and lives because money represents our work and effort.

Grace-based giving is all about knowing what Jesus has already done for us and releasing a practical expression of our faith in Him by releasing a portion of our finances for the purpose of blessing others. In turn, we receive a harvest on our seed sown and position ourselves for more to come into our hands. Giving is the believer's lifestyle and results in untold blessings when it is done from a generous heart.

Study Questions

1. Why were Paul's teachings significant when compared to other biblical writers? _____

2. The _____ realm is the only realm many Christians have not been able to conquer.

3. True or False: God is concerned with money.

4. _____ makes the Word of God of no effect.

5. True or False: There is a prosperity gospel.

6. What are we to ask about any message to determine if it is accurate? _____

7. True or False: We have the authority to determine our own harvest.

8. What indicates our level of trust in God? _____

9. Why did Jesus tell the rich young ruler to sell all his goods and give to the poor? _____

10. What is the primary purpose for employment? _____

SCRIPTURE REFERENCES

Mark 7:13

Galatians 1:1-9

2 Corinthians 9:6

Matthew 10:1, 8

1 Corinthians 16:2

Proverbs 11:25

2 Corinthians 8:2

Mark 12:41-44

Mark 10:17-24

2 Corinthians 9:10

Ephesians 4:28

Acts 20:33-35

Matthew 6:24

Luke 16:13

CHAPTER SEVENTEEN
The Giving Perspective

When we become born again, there are some things that become a reflex action. Giving is one of them. Giving is actually a response to God's unmerited, undeserved favor! When we realize how good God has been to us, we can't help but give generously. Giving ultimately stems from a revelation of the magnitude of Jesus' sacrifice for us; He was the blueprint for the giving lifestyle. There are so many things He has delivered us from that should prompt us to want to give to Him by giving to others. Some people incorrectly believe that finances have nothing to do with Christianity, but the apostle Paul taught differently. The majority of our lives are centered around obtaining money in some form or fashion. We work for it every day and need it to live in this natural world. Because God knows how integral money is to our lives, He has given us specific directions on how to handle it. Those who are still living under the law are focused on what they think they need to do to get God to bless them, but a grace-based mindset is focused on what Jesus has already done and made available to us in order to live an abundant life. Prosperity in the area of finances is a part of that.

What God is most concerned with is the condition of our hearts, not the amount that we give. The heart behind the giving is what matters. Giving joyfully, from a willing heart, pleases God and demonstrates our trust in Him. Paul regularly addressed giving as well as the necessity of staying true to the gospel that he preached, which was the Gospel of Grace. The Gospel of Grace is the message that Jesus has already done everything necessary to secure abundant life for us, independent of anything we could do on our own. This includes financial provision and blessings that enable us to live a life of abundance and be a blessing to other people through our resources. Paul said, *"I marvel that ye are so soon removed from him that called you into the grace of Christ unto another gospel: Which is not another; but there be some that trouble you, and would pervert the gospel of Christ. But though we, or an angel from heaven, preach any other gospel unto you than that which we have preached unto you, let him be accursed"* (Galatians 1:6-8). The truth is that if there were no Gospel of Grace, prosperity would not be available to any of us! We must recognize that everything good comes from God, and acknowledge when He does something for us. Psalm 118:23 says, *"This is the LORD's doing; it is marvellous in our eyes."* God's plans for us are only good.

When we realize how good God is to us, we want to give Him the praise and we want to give to others as an expression of our appreciation for what He has done for us. Please note that giving is not limited to money, but we shouldn't stop when it comes to our finances. Financial giving is a way to back up our faith and what we say we believe. It shows that we trust God without question and are willing to release whatever amount He instructs us to give. Paul taught the Corinthian church that, as they increased in every other area, they should also abound in the grace of giving (2 Corinthians 8:7). The grace to give is a supernatural ability to give in a capacity and to a degree that you wouldn't be able or desire to do in your own ability. However, when you tap into the ability of God, you can give freely and liberally without question.

GIVING: AN EXPRESSION OF TRUST

Jesus was constantly observing and testing people's hearts to see if they truly trusted God. He particularly did this in the area of giving. For example, in Mark 12:41-44, He watched people cast money into the treasury and remarked that the widow who gave her last two mites actually gave more than the wealthy people who were putting their money into the offering. The point is that this woman trusted God to such a point that she was willing to give all that she had. Even though it was a small amount monetarily, it was huge in the eyes of Jesus—even more than the large offerings of the wealthy. Her heart was in her giving; it was a sacrificial offering that was very significant to the Lord.

By comparison, Jesus' conversation with the rich young ruler revealed the heart of a man who was completely invested in his material resources and nothing else. When Jesus told him to sell all his goods and give the money to the poor, he couldn't bring himself to do it and left, saddened by Jesus' instruction (Luke 18:18-25). Everything with God boils down to the issue of trust. Jesus made it clear to His disciples that they could either serve God or money, but they couldn't serve both (Luke 16:13). This is the test that each of us will face every day—whether we will honor God with our finances or whether we will allow money to control us.

Second Corinthians 9:7, 8 reveals a key to what pleases God in the area of giving, *"Every man according as he purposeth in his heart, so let him give; not grudgingly, or of necessity: for God loveth a cheerful giver. And God is able to make all grace abound toward you; that ye, always having all sufficiency in all things, may abound to every good work."* Paul was always teaching on giving and the fact that it should never be an afterthought but a priority. We aren't to give because we are in bondage to the law, like the people were under the old covenant.

Instead, we should give because we want to, from a heart that is joyous and excited about blessing God and others through our resources. Paul also taught that we can expect a harvest when we give cheerfully, the harvest we receive will be sufficient for all our needs, and the harvest will be abundant. We have to develop faith in this area, and faith to give comes by hearing the Word of God preached on financial giving.

CONTENT IN GOD'S PROVISION

Contentment is another characteristic of a believer who is trusting in God. No matter what situation we find ourselves in, we can trust in God's provision and be content, even as we position ourselves to receive more from God. The way we position ourselves for this is through giving! Second Corinthians 9:11 says, *"Being enriched in every thing to all bountifulness, which causeth through us thanksgiving to God."* Essentially, generous giving causes others to thank God; blessing others causes them to rejoice.

To be content means to be thankful for what we do have. Paul said, *"Not that I speak in respect of want: for I have learned, in whatsoever state I am, therewith to be content. I know both how to be abased, and I know how to abound: every where and in all things I am instructed both to be full and to be hungry, both to abound and to suffer need. I can do all things through Christ which strengtheneth me"* (Philippians 4:11-13). This is the attitude we should take. Whether we have a lot or a little, we know who sustains us. Financial positions may change but God never changes, which is why putting our trust in Him is the best way to go. Paul is letting us know that we simply cannot trust in money.

First Timothy 6:6 says that godliness with contentment is great gain. It is wrong to think that our prosperity is a reflection of our godliness. Contentment and godliness go together and, when we are content in

Him, we are being godly. Money is just an added benefit of being a part of the kingdom of God and under the covenant of grace, but it should never define us or our relationship with God.

The apostle Paul was content because he had been delivered from himself, self-centeredness, selfishness, and all of the negative things that come with self-effort. He was able to preach the Gospel of Grace anywhere, even in prison. Paul was secure in who he was in Christ and knew that the most important thing a Christian could have is a strong trust in God.

Giving is truly a blessing and reflection of the character of Jesus Christ living in us. When we purpose in our hearts to give from a place of selflessness, with no motive other than to please God and bless other people, we put ourselves in a position of victory and open ourselves up to receive even more. God provides seed for those who have decided to make giving a lifestyle and ensures that we have a continual flow of finances and resources to give. This is the grace of giving personified!

Study Questions

1. True or False: Giving is a reflex action for the believer.

2. Why do we give? _____
   _____

3. True or False: Finances have nothing to do with the kingdom of God.

4. What attitude pleases God? _____

5. The only true gospel is the Gospel of _____.

6. Why is financial giving important? _____
   _____

7. Why did Jesus test people in the area of finances? ___
   _____

8. True or False: Our motive is more important than the size of our gift.

9. We should not give out of _____.

10. True or False: We can measure our relationship with God by our level of prosperity.

11. Why was Paul so content? _____
    _____

SCRIPTURE REFERENCES

Galatians 1:6-8

Psalm 118:23

2 Corinthians 8:7

Proverbs 3:5, 6, 9

Mark 12:41-44

Luke 18:18-25

Luke 16:13

2 Corinthians 9:7, 8, 11

1 Corinthians 16:2

Malachi 3:9, 10

Romans 10:17

Philippians 4:11-13

1 Timothy 6:6

CHAPTER EIGHTEEN
Partnering with God through Giving

Grace-based giving is all about honoring what Jesus has done for us and allowing our response to be one of love and appreciation. When we experience God's unmerited favor working in our lives, we cannot help but give. His grace accomplishes things we could never do on our own, and it moves us to become generous givers. The church of Macedonia experienced it during Paul's day and they responded by giving liberally. To give liberally means seeking what we can give to someone else, rather than seeking riches for ourselves. The Macedonians heard Paul's ministry and responded to it with abundant joy. They became totally focused on what they could do to help the poor, with no concern for themselves. When our motivation to give is out of love and thanksgiving for God rather than out of fear or necessity, we demonstrate the grace of God in tangible ways that others can clearly see and it draws them to the Father. This is our objective as believers.

The church of Macedonia was a great example to us today of what it looks like to give generously and willingly. In Second Corinthians 8, we see Paul addressing these believers, *"Moreover, brethren, we do you to wit of the grace of God bestowed on the churches of Macedonia; How that in a great trial of affliction the abundance of their joy and their deep poverty abounded unto the riches of their liberality. For to their power, I bear record, yea, and beyond their power they were willing of themselves; Praying us with much intreaty that we would receive the gift, and take upon us the fellowship of the ministering to the saints"* (2 Corinthians 8:1-4). The word "wit" is used here to describe Paul's desire to testify about the Macedonians, using them as an example to inspire and motivate others. The church of Macedonia gave willingly because it had experienced God's favor. This should also be our response to God's undeserved favor toward us. Joy comes from what we know and the Macedonians obviously knew something that others did not. They had an abundance of joy even in the midst of deep poverty. They gave liberally, regardless of their financial circumstances. The Bible promises that when we do this, our souls will be enriched (Proverbs 11:25). The Macedonians were so motivated by God's grace that they actually begged for opportunities to give. They were in partnership with God and the apostle Paul as they gave from cheerful hearts of love. When we have God's love in our hearts, we simply cannot turn away from those in need and refuse to help them.

The key to remember about giving is that it is not always because it is financially convenient, but it is, spiritually, the right response to God's goodness toward us. We don't give because we are required to but because we are joyful and thankful. Jesus commissioned the disciples to heal the sick, cleanse the lepers, raise the dead, cast out devils, and freely give as we have received freely from God (Matthew 10:8). We have already received faith, knowledge, and God's love. Jesus is telling us to freely give what we have been blessed with, including money.

Paul addressed the Corinthian church in an encouraging way as well:
For as touching the ministering to the saints, it is superfluous for
me to write to you: For I know the forwardness of your mind,

for which I boast of you to them of Macedonia, that Achaia was ready a year ago; and your zeal hath provoked very many... Therefore I thought it necessary to exhort the brethren, that they would go before unto you, and make up beforehand your bounty, whereof ye had notice before, that the same might be ready, as a matter of bounty, and not as of covetousness. But this I say, He which soweth sparingly shall reap also sparingly; and he which soweth bountifully shall reap also bountifully (2 Corinthians 9:1, 2, 5, 6).

In this passage, Paul wasn't putting pressure on the Corinthians but exhorting them to give by reminding them that giving from a bountiful heart will reap a bountiful harvest. God wants us to give cheerfully, and give because we genuinely desire to be a blessing to Him and others. God's grace is what enables us to give generously, which results in a generous return, while stinginess doesn't result in any significant harvest. This is a spiritual law that will work for anyone who chooses to get involved with it.

Under the Law of Moses, giving was mandatory and, if the people didn't give tithes and offerings, there was a curse attached (Malachi 3:10). Under the new covenant of grace, we are no longer under a curse or required to give "or else." Under grace, the motive for our giving is simply because we love and appreciate God and what Jesus has done for us. We don't have to give, first, in order to be blessed because God has *already* blessed us when we receive Christ. Our giving is a way for us to express grace. Gratitude is the language that God understands and responds to. As we develop our faith in the grace of God and cultivate a love relationship with the Father, we will become more sensitive to opportunities to give and bless others with our substance. In doing so, we partner with God to become the ultimate force of love toward mankind.

Study Questions

1. When we experience _____, we cannot help but to give.

2. What does it mean to give liberally? _____

3. What was significant about the Macedonian church? _____

4. How do we demonstrate the grace of God in a tangible way? _____

5. Why did the Macedonians give willingly? _____

6. What is the result of liberal giving on the soul? _____

7. True or False: Giving is included in the Great Commission.

8. God's _____ enables our giving.

9. True or False: Bad things will happen to us if we do not tithe.

10. _____ is the language of grace.

SCRIPTURE REFERENCES

2 Corinthians 8:1-24

Proverbs 11:25

Matthew 10:8

2 Corinthians 9:1-15

Malachi 3:10

1 John 3:17

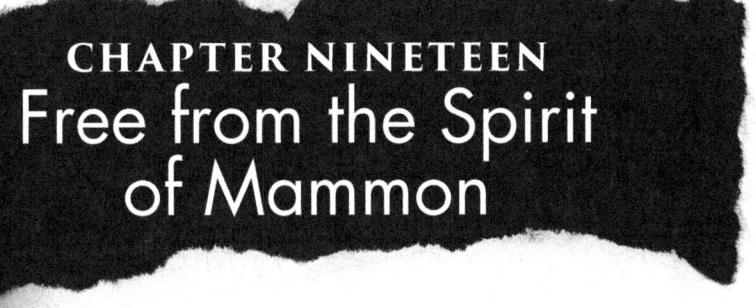

CHAPTER NINETEEN
Free from the Spirit of Mammon

The spirit of mammon is running rampant in the world. It is the spirit that is behind greed, compromise, and all manner of evil, especially as it relates to money. Unfortunately, many people have the wrong idea about money and how they should relate to the financial realm. Religion has almost made it taboo to even discuss finances in many churches, but the Bible gives us clear instructions on its use. If we are not thoroughly familiar with what the Scriptures say in this area, we can be fooled. Looking at money through the wrong lens can make it seem as if accumulating wealth is more important than anything else, but examining it with a grace-based perspective changes everything. There is nothing wrong with being wealthy as long as wealth and riches are not our central focus. Trusting and focusing on God, not money, helps us to be content in any circumstance.

The spirit of mammon is the spirit that controls this world system. It is opposed to the spirit of God and everything godly. It is a spirit that will lie to us and try to convince us that money can satisfy us on a deeper level; but this simply isn't true. Money can never give us what God can.

Many people preach what they call the gospel, but if it is something other than what the apostle Paul preached, it is not the gospel: *"I marvel that ye are so soon removed from him that called you into the grace of Christ unto another gospel: Which is not another; but there be some that trouble you, and would pervert the gospel of Christ...But I certify you, brethren, that the gospel which was preached of me is not after man. For I neither received it of man, neither was I taught it, but by the revelation of Jesus Christ"* (Galatians 1:6, 7, 11, 12).

Paul taught never to trust in money, only in God. To trust in money is actually to operate under the spirit of mammon and is counterproductive to what God wants us to experience. All money has either the Spirit of God or the spirit of mammon on it. If we do not consciously choose to rely on God to direct all of our financial dealings, we will automatically choose to operate under the spirit of mammon. Those who are being controlled by this spirit are the ones who are fearful about money and constantly in bondage to the pursuit of it, even if it involves compromising their values, morals, or principles. The spirit of mammon promises us things that only God can give.

One way to combat the spirit of mammon is to cultivate a spirit of contentment with whatever state in which you find yourself. Paul did this: *"Not that I speak in respect of want: for I have learned, in whatsoever state I am, therewith to be content. I know both how to be abased, and I know how to abound: every where and in all things I am instructed both to be full and to be hungry, both to abound and to suffer need. I can do all things through Christ which strengtheneth me"* (Philippians 4:11-13). To be content means to be thankful for what you have, with no thought of what you do not have. Contentment does not come naturally; we must work at it and learn to be content. Things like depression and discontentment constantly threaten to disrupt the contentment that God wants us to have, which is why we have to push back against these things through meditation on the Word of God. When we allow God to be our source, however, and focus on what Jesus has accomplished for us, we will find ourselves walking in the contentment that Paul spoke about. Great gain results in our lives when we mix contentment with a godly lifestyle (1 Timothy 6:6).

DON'T LOVE MONEY

The idea that money is the root of all evil is a religious one that simply isn't true. The truth is that the *love* of money is at the root of all evil. Developing a wrong relationship with the material realm is the problem. When we start to love things, instead of using things to love people, we set ourselves up for destruction.

Hebrews teaches how to cultivate an attitude of contentment and stay free from the love of money:

> Let your character *or* moral disposition be free from love of money [including greed, avarice, lust, and craving for earthly possessions] and be satisfied with your present [circumstances and with what you have]; for He [God] Himself has said, I will not in any way fail you *nor* give you up *nor* leave you without support. [I will] not, [I will] not, [I will] not in any degree leave you helpless *nor* forsake *nor* let [you] down (relax My hold on you)! [Assuredly not!] (Hebrews 13:5, 6, *AMPC*).

Contentment does not mean settling for bad circumstances. Even when we don't like where we are in life, it's important to remember that we will not stay there. It is just temporary. The love of money is the tendency to trust in money more than we trust God, which is not good. It is okay to have money but we should never start lusting after it and trying to get it by any means necessary.

God wants us to live well, but He doesn't want things to have us. We can look to Jesus as our example to see that He was well provided for at all times and flowed in financial and material resources. Even though religion portrays Jesus as poor and homeless, and claims that in order to be like Him we need to be poor, these are myths that are unscriptural. Matthew 9:1 and Mark 2:1 both let us know that Jesus was not homeless, as religion would have us believe, but that He actually had a home and a place to stay. In addition, when Jesus was crucified, He was wearing expensive clothes. His clothes were of such quality that the soldiers were casting lots for them (Matthew 27:35). This would not have been the case if Jesus' garments were cheaply made. Evidence of Jesus being of the lineage of royalty was when the wise men brought Him gold, frankincense, and myrrh.

The Bible instructs us not to let the spirit of mammon drive us to crave money and material things because doing so sets us up for disaster. Succumbing to the lust for money opens the door to many hurtful snares and temptations that can destroy a person's soul. Trusting in anything God has created rather than trusting in the Creator, Himself, is a sure way to move away from the will of God. When we put all of our trust in Jesus, the grace of God, and His finished works, we can be sure that we are on track for a life of abundance and prosperity. We will be in a place of blessing so that we can bless others and fulfill God's covenant in the earth. Freedom from the spirit of mammon is the key to being trusted with more resources from God so that we can be distribution centers and demonstrate to the world that He is a God of provision and increase.

Study Questions

1. True or False: Money is the root of all evil.

2. What enables us to be content in any circumstance? _____
   _____

3. What is the spirit of mammon? _____
   _____

4. What did Paul teach about money? _____
   _____
   _____

5. True or False: All money has either the Spirit of God or the spirit of mammon on it.

6. What does it mean to be content? _____
   _____
   _____

7. Depression and discontentment center around _____.

8. Great gain results when we mix _____
   with a _____.

9. True or False: It is okay to have money.

10. True or False: Jesus was homeless and poor.

SCRIPTURE REFERENCES

Galatians 1:6-13

Philippians 4:11-13

1 Timothy 6:6

Hebrews 13:5, 6, *AMPC*

Matthew 9:1

Mark 2:1

Matthew 27:35

Revelation 18:1-24

Matthew 8:20

Matthew 2:11

1 Timothy 6:9, 10, 17-19, *AMPC*

CHAPTER TWENTY
How to Be Free from Mammon

When we study the issue of money and how it relates to trust, we cannot ignore the presence of mammon. Mammon is an evil spirit that is never far from money; it tempts us to trust money instead of God. The parable of the unfaithful steward illustrates that this spirit is responsible for causing us to be unfaithful to God, particularly as it relates to our finances and possessions (Luke 16:1-13). Mammon is the name of the false god of riches in the Old Testament that the people served, and it is still in operation today. It causes us to put other things and other people before God, bringing us into full-blown idolatry. While money is neither righteous nor unrighteous, when mammon exerts its influence on money, it becomes destructive and actually leads us away from the will of God for our lives. We must be aware of how this demonic spirit operates so that we can fight it when it shows up.

God does not want us to trust in money or material possessions. When we find ourselves putting our trust in what's in our bank accounts, we have to recognize that the spirit of mammon is trying to influence us. Jesus taught that those who are faithful with their money will also be faithful with the weightier matters of the kingdom of God, things like healing, deliverance, the gifts of the Spirit, and more. The money test must be passed, however, in order to experience higher levels of God's power working in our lives. We cannot serve God *and* mammon, which is why we have to make a decision that we are absolutely going to trust God in every single area of our lives. Jesus referred to money as the least of all things in the kingdom of God (Luke 16:10-14), which is why believers have to master this vital area.

Unfortunately, many in the body of Christ are controlled by the spirit of mammon, but God wants His people to be set free from it. We can learn a lot about someone by observing how they handle money. Jesus made a note of this on different occasions. He watched people put money in the treasury and noticed a woman who gave all that she had (Mark 12:41-44). While there were very wealthy people giving money, this woman's offering caught Jesus' attention. Why? It was because she gave all that was in her possession. Even though it was a small amount in the eyes of the rich, in Jesus' eyes it was a substantial offering. You see, it is one thing to give a large amount when it doesn't really cost you anything, but when you give your very last, it shows you truly trust God. This is the type of heart that is completely free from mammon's influence. Matthew 6:21 addresses the heart-condition of a person as it relates to money when it says, *"For where your treasure is, there will your heart be also."*

So how do you know if the spirit of mammon is influencing you? One of the first ways you can tell is that you feel money and the pursuit of money is your first priority in life. There are people who truly believe that money is the key to their happiness and that if they aren't working hard to secure as much money as possible, they are going to lose out. This is a lie from the pit of hell and the spirit of Satan is behind it. Mammon is constantly lying to us and telling us the opposite of what God says. This spirit wants to influence us in opposition to God's Word until it gets us to believe and then say we don't need God because we have money. This is mammon's ultimate goal. Always remember that the money you possess is going to be under the same influence of whatever spirit is governing *your* life. So if mammon rules your life, your money will be ruled by mammon. If the Spirit of God rules your life, your money will be controlled by the Spirit of God. There is no in-between. You will either serve God or mammon with your money and with your life.

COMBAT MAMMON WITH THE WORD OF GOD

Like any lie from the devil, the way to combat the lies mammon tells and sells is to know and apply the Word of God. People have been led to believe that money is the root of all evil but that simply isn't true. According to the Word of God, the *love* of money is the problem (1 Timothy 6:10). God wants us to be financially blessed in the same way that Abraham, Isaac, and Solomon were blessed, but He doesn't want our possessions to rule our lives and draw us away from trusting in Him, alone.

One thing that mammon tries to do is get us into pride, which is an overestimation of ourselves and our abilities. It is also a refusal to submit to God and His way of doing things. Lucifer allowed pride to move him into a place of rebellion against God and it cost him his position in the kingdom of God. When he made his objective to be like God, he was kicked out of heaven: *"How art thou fallen from heaven, O Lucifer, son of the morning! how art thou cut down to the ground, which didst weaken the nations! For thou hast said in thine heart, I will ascend into heaven, I will exalt my throne above the stars of God: I will sit also upon the mount of the congregation, in the sides of the north: I will ascend above the heights of the clouds; I will be like the most High. Yet thou shalt be brought down to hell, to the sides of the pit"* (Isaiah 14:12-15).

No one can be God, except God. The anointing that comes from Him, alone, removes burdens and destroys yokes (Isaiah 10:27). Satan tries to use money as a negative anointing in the same manner that God uses His power positively. What the enemy is trying to do is move people into a place of thinking that the more money they have, the more they become all-powerful and almost god-like. The world equates money with power, and people do use it to try to exert control and fix their problems. However, when those people are dominated by the spirit of mammon, the end result is the exact opposite of true power. Money cannot provide you with the anointing that supernaturally delivers and sets people free. Only God can.

Trusting in God and His Word is the key to breaking free from the spirit of mammon. God is the God of hope, and Nehemiah 8:10 says the joy of the Lord is our strength. We must make a decision to choose *God* as our source, not money; *the Spirit of God*, not the spirit of mammon. To try to operate in both will lead to double-mindedness and instability that doesn't get any results (James 1:6-8). We must fight against this wicked spirit so that it doesn't mislead us.

As believers, it is so vital that we turn away from the spirit that controls this world system if we don't want to come under its influence. First John 2:15-17 says, *"Love not the world, neither the things that are in the world. If any man love the world, the love of the Father is not in him. For all that is in the world, the lust of the flesh, and the lust of the eyes, and the pride of life, is not of the Father, but is of the world. And the world passeth away, and the lust thereof: but he that doeth the will of God abideth for ever."* The "world" does not mean creation; it refers to an environment that encourages greed, a craving for everything we see, and a reliance on earthly possessions. All of these things will one day cease to exist, but God's Word will stand forever, which is why it is what we should anchor our lives to for provision, strength, power, joy, and success.

For the Christian, there are four questions we must ask ourselves to assess if the spirit of mammon is influencing us. The answers you discover will allow you to see where you need to make adjustments and renew your mind to evict this spirit out of your life for good. Consider these questions in locating whether the spirit of mammon is in operation:

1. Do I look to God or people to meet my needs?
2. Do I blame others for my present circumstances?
3. When people fail to help me the way I wanted to be helped, do I get angry or upset?
4. Will I ever have enough?

If you are born again, your only source is God. Even though we know this to be true, it often takes some serious mind renewal to live a life that is fully submitted to the truth of God as the provider of everything you need. When things look like they are scarce or when there is lack, it is easy to fall prey to the spirit of mammon which tries to push fear and anxiety over how your needs will be met. However, a consistent focus on God's Word and meditating on the Scriptures about God's love and provision will help you to stay focused on the truth of His ability and power, versus relying on your own. Any time we try to make something outside of God be our source, whether it is a person, a job, money, or ourselves, we are going to fall short. But when we lean on God for everything, we will find things flowing into our lives with less stress and toil.

God didn't create us to trust in our ability or the money that we possess. He is responsible for us and takes great delight in taking care of our needs. He wants us to have money, but He doesn't want our relationship with money to be perverted. Choose to trust Him, alone, and be released from the influence of mammon. The life God designed for you to live is waiting for you when you put money in its proper perspective and access His grace for provision that is available through the finished works of Jesus Christ.

Study Questions

1. What does mammon tempt us to do? _____

2. What is mammon? _____

3. What happens when mammon exerts its influence on money?
   _____

4. Why must the money test be passed? _____
   _____

5. Jesus referred to money as the _____ of all things in the kingdom of God.

6. How do you know mammon has influenced you? _____
   _____

7. The money you possess is going to be under the influence of _____.
   _____.

8. True or False: Money is the root of all evil.

9. What is the key to breaking free from the spirit of mammon?
   _____

10. When are you susceptible to falling prey to mammon? _____
    _____

SCRIPTURE REFERENCES

Luke 16:1-14

Mark 12:41-44

Matthew 6:21

1 Timothy 6:10

Isaiah 14:12-15

Isaiah 10:27

Nehemiah 8:10

James 1:6-8

1 John 2:15-18

Luke 6:38

Psalm 30:5

CHAPTER TWENTY-ONE
Freedom from Mammon

God wants us to be free from the spirit of mammon, and we can be when we understand exactly how it operates. The spirit of mammon has one main goal and it is to lure us away from trusting God. It tries to worm its way into every area of our lives, from our finances to our attitudes, telling us everything that is in direct opposition to the Word of God. Mammon says money is the answer to our problems and wants to convince us that it can give us what only God can give. This demonic spirit influences people to lie, cheat, steal, and compromise their values for the almighty dollar. It is prevalent in every sector of society and always has been. If we allow it to, mammon will generate fear in us about our money while convincing us that we need to go into debt to have the things we need and desire. To put it simply: mammon wants to rule our lives. The good news is that we do not have to be ruled by the spirit of mammon. We can remain free from it by trusting God, acknowledging Him daily, and being generous givers. These three things allow us to walk in the blessings of God and avoid the traps of Satan.

The Bible says that no servant can serve two masters, for either he will hate the one and love the other, or he will hold to the one and despise the other. You simply cannot serve God and mammon (Luke 16:13). Money, in and of itself, is neither good nor bad; what matters is the influence that is on our lives when money comes into our hands. If we are ruled by the spirit of the world, which is mammon, our money will be ruled by mammon. If we are ruled by the Spirit of God, our money will be used for godly purposes. Mammon wants us to trust in money rather than God. People who are heavily influenced by it are going to be governed by a spirit of fear, which will lead to more compromise and unscrupulous behavior. To be free from the spirit of mammon, we must trust God, need God, and give to God. This is what it means to honor Him.

Since staying free from mammon's influence is so critical to the lives of Christians, we need to be equipped with all the knowledge we can get. There are five things we can do to maintain our freedom from mammon. First, we must trust in God and acknowledge Him in everything. *"Trust in the LORD with all thine heart; and lean not unto thine own understanding. In all thy ways acknowledge him, and he shall direct thy paths"* (Proverbs 3:5, 6). To trust in the Lord is to rely on Him confidently in every situation. This principle works in all areas of our lives, from our health to our finances. We can choose to trust in our own understanding and allow ourselves to be moved into self-preservation, or we can trust God. A person who does not trust God with their finances is someone who thinks they are their own source of prosperity. God will keep us in perfect peace if we trust *Him* (Isaiah 26:3).

Second, we have to decide that we are not going to be wise in our own eyes. *"Be not wise in thine own eyes: fear the LORD, and depart from evil. It shall be health to thy navel, and marrow to thy bones"* (Proverbs 3:7, 8). When we do this, we will experience health and prosperity. The fear of God is basically having an attitude of honor and respect toward Him and His Word. It causes us to gain knowledge and when we are operating in the fear of the Lord, when the spirit of mammon tries to seduce us we will respect God too much to allow ourselves to be swayed. This will keep us above mammon's influence.

Third, we must honor the Lord with our substance and the first fruits of our increase. *"Honour the LORD with thy substance, and with the firstfruits of all thine increase: So shall thy barns be filled with plenty, and thy presses shall burst out with new wine. My son, despise not the chastening of the LORD; neither be weary of his correction: For whom the LORD loveth he correcteth; even as a father the son in whom he delighteth"* (Proverbs 3:9-12). Doing so causes us not only to experience increase and promotion, but it keeps us free from the spirit of mammon. We put God in first place when we allow our money to carry more weight in His kingdom than in the world. When we honor Him with our finances, He will honor us in return.

Fourth, we must purpose in our hearts to find wisdom. *"Happy is the man that findeth wisdom, and the man that getteth understanding"* (Proverbs 3:13). Wisdom has already been made available, but we must seek it out in God's Word. Keep in mind there is a difference between wisdom and knowledge; wisdom is the ability to *use* knowledge. It is like a light that shines on information, giving you insight on what to do at any given time. Wisdom is precious and far outweighs anything mammon could ever present to us. The merchandise of wisdom is better than the merchandise of silver or gold (Proverbs 3:14-16). Wisdom's ways are pleasant and her paths are peace; that is the opposite of the path mammon will take us down, which is not peaceful. Many people do not choose God because mammon seduced them before they could see what God could do. That's what mammon does; it tries to get us into discontent so that we will curse our own blessings, but godliness with contentment is great gain (1 Timothy 6:6).

Finally, we are to not withhold good from them to whom it is due, when it is in our power to do so (Proverbs 3:27). If we have been blessed and are able to bless others, we should do it. Mammon will cause us to withhold blessings, but we can overcome this spirit by deciding to be a blessing to others with our resources. To be a blessing means to be an instrument through which God flows His favor to reach someone else. It also means to prevent misfortune in someone else's life.

MAMMON COMES WITH PRIDE AND POVERTY

The spirit of mammon never operates alone, and is usually accompanied by the spirits of poverty and pride. The spirit of poverty causes a state of constantly wanting, but never having enough. It causes us to feel guilt and shame for the blessings we do have and tries to get us to hide what God is doing in our lives. This is all the work of mammon. It also causes people to hoard whatever they have and doesn't want them to know that God is able to make all grace abound to every good work (2 Corinthians 9:8).

The spirit of pride, which works with the spirit of poverty under the direction of mammon, is just as dangerous. It kills our ability to obey God and follow His plans for our lives. Proud people will not submit to God. In fact, pride causes people to turn away from Him and seek self-satisfaction; it turns people into their own gods.

God instructs us to cast all our cares on Him for He cares for us. If we refuse to do so and insist on carrying the load of our own burdens rather than giving them to God, we will not find the grace to deal with the issues of life. We must choose whom we will serve and reject the suggestions of mammon to rely on our own effort and ability to take care of ourselves and our needs without God.

You can experience freedom from the spirit of mammon forever by putting into practice the five action steps to maintaining this freedom and remaining consistent in executing them. Not only will you find yourself growing in your relationship with God, but you will begin to experience increase in many arenas of your life. Mammon has no power in the life of a Christian who honors God, first, in his or her finances and obeys God's instructions.

Study Questions

1. What is mammon's main goal? _____
   _____

2. What does this spirit influence people to do? _____
   _____

3. True or False: You can serve God and mammon.

4. If we are ruled by the Spirit of God, our money will be used for ___
   _____.

5. Mammon wants us to trust in _____.

6. What five things must we do to maintain our freedom from mammon? _____
   _____
   _____

7. Mammon is accompanied by the spirits of _____ and
   _____.

8. True or False: The spirit of poverty tries to get us to feel guilty about our blessings.

9. The spirit of pride kills our ability to _____.

10. What happens when we don't cast our cares on God? _____
    _____

SCRIPTURE REFERENCES

Luke 16:13

Proverbs 3:5-20, 27

Isaiah 26:3

1 Timothy 6:6, 10

2 Corinthians 9:8

Galatians 6:7

Proverbs 3:5-20, 27

Isaiah 53:5

Philippians 4:19

Proverbs 1:7

1 Peter 5:7

Joshua 24:15

CHAPTER TWENTY-TWO
Choose God or Mammon

Money is an extremely hot topic in the body of Christ for a number of reasons. First, religion has given us the idea that money is negative in and of itself and that it should be avoided in the lives of Christian people. The idea that God actually desires His people to prosper is taboo amongst many believers. There are also those Christians whose lives are controlled by the spirit of mammon and who have given in to a spirit of greed, covetousness, and obsession with possessions. Both of these ways of relating to money are wrong. When Jesus talked about money, He also referred to the spirit of mammon that can become attached to it. The issue God wants us to understand is that we cannot serve Him and serve mammon at the same time—we must choose one or the other. The Christian's responsibility is to serve God as a conscious choice, which keeps us from becoming enslaved by the wicked spirit of mammon. When we try to serve God and mammon, double-mindedness and instability will be the result. The spirit of mammon wants to keep us in debt, both financially and spiritually, but when we apply the Word of God in every area of our lives, we declare war on mammon and rebel against it. We can overcome it by deliberately choosing to submit to the Word of God.

God's will does not include His people going in debt, particularly to get our needs met. In the microwave society in which we live, and especially when we go through times in life when we want or need something, it is easy to go into debt. However, going into debt to acquire the things you desire or need in the moment is a decision that is driven by the spirit of mammon. Jesus taught many times about money and the foundational concept that He was communicating to those listening was that faithfulness in the financial arena sets the tone for faithfulness in greater things in the kingdom of God. He also taught that it is impossible to serve both God and mammon; you must choose one or the other (Luke 16:10-13).

One example of serving mammon is going into debt. It is no secret that debt controls many people's lives and actually becomes the ultimate bondage that brings stress, anxiety, and fear. This is why God doesn't want us going into financial debt if we can avoid it. Once you get caught in the debt trap, it is difficult to break out. Some of us need supernatural help to break free from debt, and that help is available. We are not children of the natural realm, but of the supernatural realm (Galatians 4:22-31). Because of this, we have access to supernatural debt-cancellation.

The Word gives powerful examples of debt cancellation in the lives of those who trusted God. In Second Kings, we see the example of a man recovering a borrowed axe head that had fallen into the water: *"But as one was felling a beam, the axe head fell into the water: and he cried, and said, Alas, master! for it was borrowed. And the man of God said, Where fell it? And he shewed him the place. And he cut down a stick, and cast it in thither; and the iron did swim. Therefore said he, Take it up to thee. And he put out his hand, and took it"* (2 Kings 6:5-7). We know that iron does not naturally float but, through the supernatural power of God, the axe head floated to the surface and was able to be recovered. God released supernatural means in this scenario to rescue this man from a debt that he would have owed. The same is true today! God's debt-cancelling power is available to all who desire to be free from the bondage of debt and avoid the control of mammon in their finances.

The borrower is a servant to the lender (Proverbs 22:7). This is another reason why God doesn't want us to be in debt—it puts us in the position of being a servant to the one from whom we borrowed. When we buy things on credit that we know we can't afford to pay back right away, we subject ourselves to the tyranny of those lenders with whom we entered into an agreement. This gives the spirit of mammon free reign to push us down and keep us from making any financial progress.

Mammon is all about stopping us in our tracks, while God wants to move us forward. It is a spirit that will use us up, then convince us that we would be better off dying rather than continue on with God. The reason mammon wants to paralyze us is because it does not want us to get out of the "drought" seasons of our lives. If it can keep us in a perpetual wilderness, we will never see the will of God come to pass. Forward momentum is exactly what the spirit of mammon wants to hinder in the life of a Christian.

The Word of God has wonderful examples of people who overcame the challenges they faced and kept moving forward despite opposition. Isaac is one such example. Isaac sowed in the land where he lived and reaped a great harvest as a result, even though there was a severe drought taking place in that region: *"Then Isaac sowed in that land, and received in the same year an hundredfold: and the Lord blessed him. And the man waxed great, and went forward, and grew until he became very great"* (Genesis 26:12, 13). Have you ever been in the middle of what appeared to be a drought in your life? It is during those times that God wants you to demonstrate faithfulness with your finances and continue to give to His kingdom; it is also during those times that the spirit of mammon will come to you and try to stop you from doing so. We can learn from Isaac's life what happens when you rebel against the spirit of mammon and sow anyway. God honors you when you trust Him to provide for your needs and give of what you do have, believing that a harvest will come to you. There is no drought or natural circumstance that can stop the faith and obedience of a believer who trusts God.

Jesus is our primary example of how to press past the spirit of mammon even when faced with challenges. Remember, the spirit of mammon opposes the will of God, so it will try to influence your attitude to make you want to quit on God. Jesus refused to quit in the midst of an agonizing situation in the garden of Gethsemane before He went to the cross: "*...Father, if thou be willing, remove this cup from me: nevertheless not my will, but thine, be done. And there appeared an angel unto him from heaven, strengthening him. And being in an agony he prayed more earnestly: and his sweat was as it were great drops of blood falling down to the ground*" (Luke 22:42-44). Jesus trusted God and kept moving forward despite the temptation to quit when things got hard.

Another tactic the spirit of mammon uses is attempting to use our past against us. The Word of God is critical to combating this strategy of the enemy against our lives. When the devil tries to throw your past in your face, remind him that the Scriptures say God does not remember the former things, neither does He consider the things of old. He promises to do a new thing in our lives when we receive Christ. He promises to make a way out of no way and water our dry places (Isaiah 43:18, 19). We all have issues in our past that the enemy tries to remind us of, but we have to make a decision to let them go and move on. God has too much in store for us to focus on what is behind us; He has removed those old things from us and cast them as far as the east is from the west (Psalm 103:12). Whatever we did in the past could never outdo what God has done and is currently doing in our present. Any sin that abounded in our lives only qualifies us for more of God's grace!

Even though the spirit of mammon will try to pull us back into the old lifestyles and ways of doing things that we embraced before coming to the knowledge of the truth, we have been empowered by grace, through faith, to forget the things that try to haunt us from our past. We will not press forward without opposition and must remember this at all times. Mammon is that opposition and we must remain on guard against it. It will try to seduce us into cursing our inheritance. It will try to get us to activate its curses against our portion by causing discontent, murmuring, and complaining. These are the times that the Word of God must rise up within us to push back mammon's advances.

The spirit of discontent is born out of mammon, but God teaches us to be content in any situation. Philippians 4:11-13 says, *"Not that I speak in respect of want: for I have learned, in whatsoever state I am, therewith to be content. I know both how to be abased, and I know how to abound: every where and in all things I am instructed both to be full and to be hungry, both to abound and to suffer need. I can do all things through Christ which strengtheneth me."* Paul had to learn how to be content. This takes time, discipline, and a commitment to focus on God no matter what the circumstance may be. We must always be in the process of learning to be content. Contentment is thankfulness for what we have, without thinking of what we do not have.

The Word of God says to be on guard against covetousness, which also breeds discontent. When you start meditating on what you do not have, which is the job of mammon, you will begin to become obsessed with obtaining those things. God doesn't want us getting into covetousness or discontent; instead He wants us to realize that He will never leave or forsake us (Hebrews 13:5). He takes care of us and provides all our needs and desires, giving us exactly what we need when we need it. In fact, those times in our lives when we appear to have less than what we would like to have are actually character-building times. Proverbs says it is better to have little, with righteousness, than to have large sums of money and be unrighteous (Proverbs 16:8). Again, please know that it is not that God doesn't want us to have a lot of money; He just wants our hearts, minds, and character to be in the right place. When you are content with what you have and are thriving in your relationship with God, you are a candidate for promotion. If we obtain possessions but are still in a state of discontent, it lets us know that mammon is running the show. We need to be okay with ourselves and what we have, right where we are, until it is time for us to move to the next level.

STEP INTO THE SUPERNATURAL

While mammon's job is to steal, kill, and destroy our lives, God wants us to experience His supernatural power in full operation. When we begin to step into the supernatural, we can expect four things to happen:

1. **Restoration**

God is in the business of restoration! Whatever we have lost or that has been stolen from us will be returned to us a hundred-fold when we trust God. He is a loving Father and He will not stand by and watch the enemy steal from us without repaying us. We simply have to have faith that He will do exactly what He promised.

2. **Supernatural progress**

When the supernatural power of God begins to flow in our lives, we will not have to settle for average progress in the natural realm. The world system is based on self-effort, toil, and a sense of self-reliance in order to make progress, but no amount of self-effort can compare to when God supernaturally moves you forward. Accelerated progress is a by-product of the supernatural power of God.

3. Supernatural favor

The favor of God is working on behalf of those who are in Christ at all times. Through supernatural favor, we are able to receive things for which we did not work. Doors are opened for us that we didn't earn the right to have opened, and opportunities are given to us simply because of the favor of God.

4. A change of status

When God's supernatural power is at work, there will be a change of status in your life. You will experience promotion, recognition, and new positions in various arenas of your life, whether personally or financially, that will have the signature of God all over them. When you receive the anointing of God, your old status will bow down to your new status and you will no longer be who and what you used to be. This is the result of serving God and not mammon.

Always remember that anything good that we have ever experienced or received in life came from God. We are not the source of our own prosperity as mammon would have us to believe, but God is our source. When we sow good seeds into the kingdom of God and sow the seeds of trust in Him, we will reap a harvest of supernatural provision, increase, and promotion. We will experience debt-cancellation and the wisdom we need to stay out of debt. Mammon tries to convince us that our seeds won't produce any harvest, but trust God's Word. Choose God over mammon and begin to live a flourishing life of abundance that will bring Him glory in this earth!

Study Questions

1. What does religion teach about money? _____

2. True or False: The idea that God wants His people to prosper is taboo.

3. What happens when we try to serve God and mammon? _____
   _____

4. God's will is not for us to go into _____.

5. Faithfulness in the financial arena sets the tone for faithfulness in
   _____.

6. True or False: God's ability to cancel debt is available to you today.

7. Covetousness breeds _____.

8. The spirit of mammon opposes the _____.

9. What can we expect when the supernatural power of God shows up in our lives? _____
   _____

SCRIPTURE REFERENCES

Luke 16:10-13

Galatians 4:22-31

2 Kings 6:5-7

Proverbs 22:7

Genesis 26:12, 13

Luke 22:42-44

Isaiah 43:18, 19

Psalm 103:12

Philippians 4:11-13

Hebrews 13:5

Proverbs 16:8

James 1:8

Romans 13:8

Psalm 30:5

Micah 7:19

Philippians 3:12-14

1 Timothy 6:3-7, 9, 10

Galatians 6:3, 7, 8

CHAPTER TWENTY-THREE
Godly Influence on Money

During His earthly ministry, Jesus went to great lengths to teach and explain how money and trust are intricately connected. For the believer, this is what God wants us to learn and practice: trusting God is the key to overcoming the spirit of mammon and destroying its influence in our lives. When we put our trust in our finances and material possessions, we open the door to Satan's influence. Whatever spirit influences us, whether God or mammon, will rub off on our money. If we aren't careful, we can become confused and think we can actually serve God *and* mammon, but that's impossible. Regardless of the messages mammon tries to sell us, money can never do the things that God can do. Submitting to a godly influence on our money allows us to honor God and do what He instructs us to do. Honor is the currency for promotion, expansion, and all the things we hope to see happen in our lives.

One of the most important things we must realize as believers is that God requires complete loyalty to Him if we say we are His. He doesn't want us on the fence about where our allegiance lies. The choice to serve either God or mammon is up to us but we cannot choose to serve both.

Luke 16:10-13 gives us the foundation for developing the right attitude toward money according to Jesus:

> He that is faithful in that which is least is faithful also in much: and he that is unjust in the least is unjust also in much. If therefore ye have not been faithful in the unrighteous mammon, who will commit to your trust the true riches? And if ye have not been faithful in that which is another man's, who shall give you that which is your own? No servant can serve two masters: for either he will hate the one, and love the other; or else he will hold to the one, and despise the other. Ye cannot serve God and mammon.

This passage is specifically talking about money (the least) and letting us know that if we do not submit to a godly influence on our lives in general, we will not be faithful with money. If we try to serve God and mammon at the same time, the Word of God says we are double-minded and unstable (James 1:7, 8). We are thrown into confusion when we try to mix the things of this world with the things of God. It is simply impossible to thrive when we refuse to submit to God one hundred percent. The spirit of mammon operates in the world system and we must keep ourselves separate from it.

BENEFITS OF HONORING GOD

There are many ways to combat the spirit of mammon but one of the most powerful ways is to decide to honor God with your money. This is a deliberate act of rebellion against the spirit of mammon and shuts down its operation in your life. Proverbs 3 says, *"Honour the LORD with thy substance, and with the firstfruits of all thine increase: So shall thy barns be filled with plenty, and thy presses shall burst out with new wine"* (Proverbs 3:9, 10). What a promise from God! Another word for *substance* is *capital*. This is basically telling us to honor God with our money.

To honor something is to allow it to carry weight or weigh in heavily. We honor God when we give Him first place in our lives by demonstrating that His words carry more weight than anything else. For example, if God instructs you to give a certain amount of money in church or to someone He puts on your heart to give to, you don't ask questions or use that money for something else. You obey His instructions and give. This is what it means to honor God with your money. It also means giving into the things of God before spending money on yourself, whether it is your tithes, offerings, or other financial gifts. God promises that if we honor Him, He will honor us, and no one can honor us like God can (1 Samuel 2:30; John 5:44).

The story of Jesus feeding the multitude with five barley loaves and two fish is an example of how the act of trusting in God precedes the manifestation of supernatural provision. It's also an example of how one little boy's honor for God through his small offering resulted in him benefitting from the miracle Jesus performed:

> There is a lad here who has five barley loaves and two small fishes, but what are they among so many? Jesus said, Make the men sit down. So the men sat down, in number about five thousand. Jesus took the loaves, and when he had given thanks, he distributed to the disciples, and the disciples to them that were sitting, and likewise of the fishes as much as they would. When they were filled, he said to his disciples, Gather up the fragments that remain, that nothing be lost. Therefore they gathered them together, and filled twelve baskets with the fragments of the five barley loaves, which remained over and above unto them who had eaten (John 6:9-13).

The small offering of fish and bread was sown; God blessed it and His supernatural ability activated that offering to multiply for the purpose of feeding thousands of people! Jesus didn't forget about the boy who sowed his small seed, and ensured that there was plenty left over for him to enjoy. He will do the same for us when we trust Him with our resources, no matter how little the amount may be.

The life of a Christian should be characterized by complete trust in God at all times. We do this by seeking God and His kingdom first, not money and things. Matthew 6:33 promises that when we put God first over everything and seek Him as the priority, everything else will be added to us. We should never seek things, but instead they should seek us. Promotion will search us out and find us when we honor and put God first.

Saul honored God with money:

And he said unto him, Behold now, there is in this city a man of God, and he is an honourable man; all that he saith cometh surely to pass: now let us go thither; peradvadventure he can shew us our way that we should go. Then said Saul to his servant, But, behold, if we go, what shall we bring the man? for the bread is spent in our vessels, and there is not a present to bring to the man of God: what have we? And the servant answered Saul again, and said, Behold, I have here at hand the fourth part of a shekel of silver: that will I give to the man of God, to tell us our way... And as they were going down to the end of the city, Samuel said to Saul, Bid the servant pass on before us, (and he passed on), but stand thou still a while, that I may shew thee the word of God (1 Samuel 9:6-8, 27).

Saul and his servant took something physical, in this case money, to honor God. As a result, they received a word from God.

SUPERNATURAL RESTORATION THROUGH HONORING GOD

Samuel's prophecy to Saul demonstrates what happens when the anointing of God is released through honor, as well as what happens when a person comes under a godly influence:

Then Samuel took a vial of oil, and poured it upon his head, and kissed him, and said, Is it not because the Lord hath anointed thee to be captain over his inheritance? When thou art departed from me today, then thou shalt find two men by Rachel's sepulchre in the border of Benjamin at Zelzah; and they will say unto thee, The asses which thou wentest to seek are found: and, lo, thy father hath left the care of the asses, and sorroweth for you, saying, What shall I do for my son? Then shalt thou go on forward from thence, and thou shalt come to the plain of Tabor, and there shall meet thee three men going up to God to Bethel, one carrying three kids, and another carrying three loaves of bread, and another carrying a bottle of wine: And they will salute thee, and give thee two loaves of bread; which thou shalt receive of their hands. After that thou shalt come to the hill of God, where is the garrison of the Philistines: and it shall come to pass, when thou art come thither to the city, that thou shalt meet a company of prophets coming down from the high place with a psaltery, and a tabret, and a pipe, and a harp, before them; and they shall prophesy: And the Spirit of the Lord will come upon thee, and thou shalt prophesy with them, and shalt be turned into another man (1 Samuel 10:1-6).

Oil is symbolic of the anointing of God. When godly influence is operating in our lives, the anointing will show up, just like it did for Saul. What had previously been lost was found through supernatural restoration. When the Spirit of God comes upon us our old man, which is our old nature, must bow down and submit to the new man, which is our born-again spirit.

Many people say they honor God, but their lives and actions demonstrate the exact opposite (Isaiah 29:13; Matthew 15:8). We determine where our hearts are invested by locating where our money can be found, which is why it is so important that we make sure our money is found honoring God. When we put our trust in Him and honor Him with our substance, we will not be moved by trouble or negative circumstances. The spirit of mammon will not be able to get a foothold in our lives. Neither fear of the future nor calamity will visit us because we know who our source is. By allowing God's influence to overtake our money, we will be carriers of His supernatural power, not only in the financial arena but in every area of our lives.

Study Questions

1. What does God want the believer to learn and put into practice concerning money? _____

2. What happens when we trust in money? _____

3. True or False: It is impossible to serve God and mammon.

4. God requires complete _____.

5. True or False: If we do not submit to godly influence in our lives, we will not be faithful with money.

6. What is one of the most powerful ways to combat the spirit of mammon? _____

7. What does it mean to honor something? _____

8. What is "substance"? _____

9. What does the story of Jesus feeding the multitude teach us?

10. What happens when godly influence is operating in our lives?

SCRIPTURE REFERENCES

Luke 16:10-13

James 1:7, **8**

Proverbs 3:9, 10

1 Samuel 2:30

John 5:44

John 6:9-13

1 Samuel 9:6-8, 27

1 Samuel 10:1-6

Isaiah 29:13

Matthew 15:8

Mark 2:21, 22

Revelation 3:15, 16

1 John 2:15, 16

Matthew 19:16-22

Mark 10:17-22

Luke 18:18-23

Matthew 6:21, 33

Luke 12:34

Psalm 23:1-6

Psalm 91:7

CHAPTER TWENTY-FOUR
The Pull of Mammon

There is so much to understand about the spirit of mammon in order to effectively combat it and recognize when it is trying to work its way into your life. The Bible has much to say about money and how we relate to it, which is why studying the Word of God to gain insight into how Satan pulls us into the trap of mammon is vital. When we are under the influence of this spirit, we are in a place of low-level thinking and living that will keep us from experiencing the true riches of God's abundance in our lives. The pull of mammon is a seductive one, but we have the power residing in us, through Christ, to overcome it on every front. Make no mistake about it, you cannot be led by the spirit of mammon and the Spirit of God at the same time; you must choose whom you will serve.

Satan and mammon are one and the same. It's just that mammon is one way the enemy manifests himself, specifically in the financial arena. Mammon is the influence of the spirit of the world in our financial dealings. It is designed to pull us toward the earth, rather than have us focus on God and things in the heavenly realm. Luke 16 is the foundational Scripture passage for understanding God's position on mammon:

> He that is faithful in that which is least is faithful also in much: and he that is unjust in the least is unjust also in much. If therefore ye have not been faithful in the unrighteous mammon, who will commit to your trust the true riches? And if ye have not been faithful in that which is another man's, who shall give you that which is your own? No servant can serve two masters: for either he will hate the one, and love the other; or else he will hold to the one, and despise the other. Ye cannot serve God and mammon (Luke 16:10-13).

What Jesus is saying here is that you cannot be under the influence of God *and* the spirit of the world that seeks to direct your money. You are going to have to choose one or the other, but you can't serve both. God and mammon are in direct opposition to each other.

Mammon wants to strip us of God and leave us broken and alone, without any other hope than mammon itself. Mammon has an abusive quality to it, seeking to isolate us from God and rely on it, alone, as our source. It traps us into thinking that it can provide what we need to be taken care of and that we have no other options. Debt is a perfect example of the spirit of mammon in operation, with its rules and penalties for violating the terms and conditions of the lender's agreement. Mammon seeks to bind us in situations that become increasingly difficult to get out of and that require more and more of mammon's assistance. It is always pulling us low and trying to teach us its ways rather than God's ways.

When the spirit of mammon is confronting you and attempting to get you to yield to the lie that it is qualified to take care of your needs, it is critical to put yourself in remembrance of God's power. The psalmist said, *"I will lift up mine eyes unto the hills, from whence cometh my help. My help cometh from the* LORD, *which made heaven and earth"* (Psalm 121:1, 2). What makes God qualified to lead your life? The fact that He created heaven and earth! The spirit of mammon is no match for God and His ability. While mammon wants you to factor in everything other than God's ability when things look like they are going wrong, God wants you to look *only* to Him as your source of assistance. Mammon wants you to consider your income and make decisions around what your bank account balance is showing you, while God wants you to receive the truth that there are no limits in Him. He is able to do exceedingly above all you could ask or think when you trust Him alone (Ephesians 3:20). You are not disqualified from divine intervention, even though mammon tries to convince you otherwise. The power of God's anointing is available to all who are in expectation of Him showing up in their situation.

DISCERNING THE VOICE OF MAMMON

There are many voices speaking to us all the time. The Word of God is the key to sharpening our spiritual discernment so that we can identify when the spirit of mammon is speaking to us (Hebrews 4:12). Whenever we are facing a decision or situation, and we think we are hearing an instruction or a suggestion, the first thing we need to do is ask ourselves whether it is the spirit of mammon or the Spirit of God speaking to us. There are a several checkpoints you can set up to determine what you are hearing. The following are characteristics of the voice of mammon:

1. Mammon pulls us out of the flow of divine thought and disregards the Word of God on provision.
2. Mammon falsely suggests that your stability is tied to what is going on in your finances.
3. Mammon implies that when you get money or your needs are met, you can relax your faith as it relates to trusting in God.
4. Mammon pulls us away from the voice of the Spirit of God and pushes us toward the voice of man's reason.

5. Mammon pushes us toward the flesh and holds us in a place of containment.
6. Mammon places financial outcomes and financial advantages ahead of God's desire.
7. Mammon always appeals to our sense of gain or loss.
8. Mammon attempts to control the direction/flow of your money above the direction of God.
9. Mammon is tied to the fear of lack and convinces you that you need to do something connected to this world system in order to secure your provision.
10. Mammon wants to lower your gaze to focus on what people have done to you or haven't done for you.

If you find yourself yielding to any of these suggestions, you can be sure that the spirit of mammon is speaking to you.

God's desire for each of us is that we live an abundant life where all of our needs and desires are taken care of by Him. Through Jesus Christ, we can live like Adam and Eve did in the garden of Eden, with God as our source for everything. There is no prosperity in considering what mammon says or suggests. When we choose to trust God entirely, we will experience a level of freedom in our finances that only goes to greater levels. The pull of mammon is no match for a believer who is submitted to God's Word and voice in every situation and circumstance he or she faces. No matter what is going on in your life, trust God and choose to follow His way of doing things. Abandon the spirit of the world system and your own efforts as your means of provision and plug into the eternal provision of God. Mammon will have no choice but to submit!

Study Questions

1. When we are under the influence of mammon, we are in a place of low-level _____ and _____.

2. True or False: You cannot be led by God and mammon.

3. True or False: Satan and mammon are one and the same.

4. What is mammon? _____

5. Mammon wants to pull us toward the _____.

6. Mammon seeks to _____ us from God.

7. What is the key to sharpening our spiritual discernment?

8. True or False: When your needs are taken care of, you can relax your faith in God as your source.

9. What fear is mammon tied to? _____

10. Mammon always appeals to our sense of _____ or _____.

SCRIPTURE REFERENCES

Luke 16:10-13

Psalm 121:1, 2

Ephesians 3:20

Hebrews 4:12

CHAPTER TWENTY-FIVE
Conquering the Spirit of Mammon: A Five-Step Process

Conquering the Spirit of Mammon: A Five-Step Process

Many times, Christians forget who they are and think they need to fight the devil in order to get victory in their lives. The truth is that Satan has already been defeated, and our spiritual warfare revolves around reminding ourselves who we are in Christ when the devil tries to tell us otherwise. The spirit of mammon is constantly seeking inroads into our lives. It is designed to lure us away from our trust in God and His provision. When we as believers are not established in our Christ-identity, we become susceptible to believing the lies of mammon. However, when we apply five key steps to conquering the spirit of mammon, we can walk in the victory that Jesus has already secured for us as it relates to the financial realm. We have everything we need on the inside of us to experience total deliverance from the spirit of mammon.

There is a practical way to break free from the clutches of mammon and it involves five steps that we can implement for maximum results. The first step is to recognize and remember our identity. In other words, we must know who we are in Christ. If we are always conscious of our Christ-identity, then we know we can always win and can never be defeated. We will remain above the circumstances we face and will never get under them. In Christ, we can see things from a perspective that the world cannot see.

Second Corinthians 13:5 says, *"Examine yourselves, whether ye be in the faith; prove your own selves. Know ye not your own selves, how that Jesus Christ is in you, except ye be reprobates?"* Paul is instructing believers to examine their walk with Christ. Specifically, examine where you are in your knowledge of who you are in Him. Are you holding to the faith in who you are in Him and the power you possess as a result of Him living in you, or are you living under your circumstances? Every day we are to have an ever-increasing experience with Jesus. When we have a working revelation of who we are in Him, the spirit of mammon cannot tempt us with loss or the fear of not having enough.

Ephesians 3:8 says, *"Unto me, who am less than the least of all saints, is this grace given, that I should preach among the Gentiles the unsearchable riches of Christ."* Paul said that he was instructed by God to preach to us the unsearchable riches of Christ. This is powerful because it lets us know that we have in us unsearchable riches and untold resources! The spirit of mammon will try to tempt you with lack or loss, but those things cannot work when you know you possess unsearchable riches. When we look into the mirror of the Word of God and then walk away remembering who we are, nothing that tries to move us from our true identity will work. We are to remain in a position of constant, continual trust in Christ.

The second step to conquering the spirit of mammon is to locate where your treasure is. *"Lay not up for yourselves treasures upon earth, where moth and rust doth corrupt, and where thieves break through and steal: But lay up for yourselves treasures in heaven, where neither moth nor rust doth corrupt, and where thieves do not break through nor steal: For where your treasure is, there will your heart be also"* (Matthew 6:19-21). Your treasure can only be in one of two places: heaven or earth. We all have to locate where our treasure is because that will let us know where our hearts are invested. Colossians says, *"If ye then be risen with Christ, seek those things which are above, where Christ sitteth on the right hand of God. Set your affection on things above, not on things on the earth"* (Colossians 3:1, 2). This verse directly relates to Matthew 6:22, 23, which says that if the eye of a person is single and focused on the things of God, their whole body, or life, will be full of light, but if their eye is set on the things of the world, or darkness, darkness will envelop their life. By this, we can see that keeping our focus and affections on the things of God's kingdom is a key to staying above the earthly pull of mammon.

Step three to conquering mammon is: decide whom you are going to serve—God or mammon—because you can't serve both. Committing to God's way of doing things as the only way you are going to conduct your life is vital for staying free from mammon's clutches. This is a decision that you must settle in your life. All that is in the world system is the lust of the flesh, the lust of the eyes, and the pride of life (1 John 2:15, 16). When you give in to mammon's suggestions, you are giving in to the very spirit that is in opposition to God. The book of Matthew lets us know that we cannot be led by God and mammon (Matthew 6:24). Making a quality decision to follow God and His Word, only, will strip mammon of its influence in your life.

The fourth step to conquering the spirit of mammon is to refuse to worry about anything concerning your life. Jesus talked about anxiety and God's kingdom:

Therefore I say unto you, Take no thought for your life, what ye shall eat, or what ye shall drink; nor yet for your body, what ye shall put on. Is not the life more than meat, and the body than raiment?...Therefore take no thought, saying, What shall we eat? or, What shall we drink? or, Wherewithal shall we be clothed? (For after all these things do the Gentiles seek:) for your heavenly Father knoweth that ye have need of all these things. But seek ye first the kingdom of God, and his righteousness; and all these things shall be added unto you (Matthew 6:25, 31-33).

God doesn't want us taking any thought for how our needs are going to be met! He tells us not to worry because grace has our backs. God's grace is sufficient to cover every need and desire that we could possibly have. If He said it, His Word is true. Philippians 4:6, 7 says, *"Be careful for nothing; but in every thing by prayer and supplication with thanksgiving let your requests be made known unto God. And the peace of God, which passeth all understanding, shall keep your hearts and minds through Christ Jesus."* As believers, we are not to have fear or anxiety about *anything*. If you do, you have forgotten who is on the inside of you. No matter what you are facing, come to the conclusion that there is more working *for* you than there is working against you. When you refuse to worry and bring your requests to God with an attitude of thanksgiving, the peace of God will overtake your soul.

In the world system, there is a belief that money can buy security, but in God's system, trusting Him eradicates fear. The spirit of mammon tries to convince us that it can take care of our financial problems and provide for us, but the Spirit of God says, "I've already taken care of that."

The last step to conquering the spirit of mammon is to seek the kingdom of God and seek it *first*. Matthew 6:33 says, *"But seek ye first the kingdom of God, and his righteousness; and all these things shall be added unto you."* God has packed our spirits with so much goodness and greatness that no matter how much lack a situation tries to present to us, we will never run out. Mammon wants us to fear that we won't obtain what we need and that we will lose what we have but, in Christ, there is never any loss.

Applying these five steps to our daily lives and keeping them in remembrance will set us on the path to breaking free and remaining free from the influence of the spirit of mammon. Meditate on the Word of God and become established in who you are in Christ. This is the foundation for your victory. In Him, you have everything you will ever need to experience the abundant life of God on the earth.

Study Questions

1. What is spiritual warfare for the believer? _____
   _____

2. What are the five steps to conquering the spirit of mammon? _____
   _____
   _____

3. True or False: You can never be defeated when you know who you are in Christ.

4. In what area does God want us to examine ourselves according to Second Corinthians 13:5? _____

5. True or False: We possess the resources we need to get all our needs met.

6. The spirit of mammon tries to tempt you with _____ or _____.

7. Your treasure will be in one of two places: _____ or _____.

8. What happens when your eye is set on the things of the world?
   _____

9. True or False: Christians are not to have fear or anxiety over anything.

10. What does it mean to seek God's kingdom first? _____
    _____

SCRIPTURE REFERENCES

2 Corinthians 13:5

Ephesians 3:8

Matthew 6:19-25, 31-33

Colossians 3:1, 2

1 John 2:15, 16

Philippians 4:6, 7

James 1:22-23

1. WHAT IS MAMMON?

1. True
2. True
3. to convince us we don't need God to take care of us
4. self-effort and doing things in our own ability
5. deceitful
6. greater things in the kingdom of God
7. True
8. the very kingdoms and authority that He came to restore to mankind
9. give in to Satan's suggestions to trust in our money and material possessions
10. in the present instead of projecting our fears and worries into the future

2. MAMMON: THE SPIRIT OF SATAN

1. We miss the true meaning of what God is trying to say.
2. the importance of trusting God
3. by how he or she handles finances
4. tool
5. steal; kill; destroy
6. least
7. mammon
8. True
9. True
10. an attempt to use materials to replace God

3. UNMASKING THE SPIRIT OF MAMMON
1. Mammon is responsible for us being unfaithful to God.
2. the name of the false god of riches in the Old Testament
3. put other things and other people before God, bringing us into full-blown idolatry
4. True
5. False
6. You feel money and the pursuit of money is your first priority in life.
7. Do I look to God or people to meet my needs? Do I blame others for my present circumstances? When people fail to help me the way I wanted to be helped, do I get angry or upset? Will I ever have enough?
8. God
9. meditate on the Scriptures about God's love provision

4. THREE SPIRITS OF MAMMON
1. to get us to trust money more than God
2. when we are not well-versed in the Word
3. money; attitudes
4. spiritual things
5. our willingness to give
6. because she gave all she had
7. pride, greed, and poverty
8. be ashamed of God's blessings
9. maintaining your stance of victory in the face of contradictory circumstances
10. by acknowledging God in all your ways and purposing in your heart to live a giving lifestyle

5. MAMMON'S AGENDA

1. True
2. The spirit of mammon can attach itself to our finances.
3. to get you to abandon God as your source and trust in your money, your ability, your intellect, and your way of doing things, apart from God
4. money
5. It is the least in the kingdom of God.
6. money or riches
7. curse; disobedience
8. True
9. achievement and financial success
10. Repent for allowing money to have your heart and soul, and acknowledge God as your only source.

6. THE TACTICS OF MAMMON

1. fear
2. It makes Christians afraid to have money.
3. False
4. because they were greedy and afraid that people would stop giving them money when they learned the truth
5. traditions
6. the norms, values, and beliefs of society that oppose the Word of God
7. It always opposes God's will.
8. They were motivated by the spirit of mammon.
9. False
10. True

7. THE OPERATION OF THE SPIRIT OF MAMMON

1. by hiding himself
2. They reject any message on finances.
3. trusting God
4. by how we handle financial matters
5. sow; reap
6. servants
7. False
8. It will destroy you.
9. It can protect us from our problems, it can provide what only God can, and that we need to acquire more money.
10. to teach us that He is the source of our prosperity, not ourselves

8. THE SNEAKY SPIRIT OF MAMMON

1. to cause us to serve it
2. money
3. True
4. God; mammon
5. money
6. False
7. to make Him your priority in every area of your life
8. security, significance, identity, power, freedom, and self-esteem
9. by placing our trust in God and meditating on His Word
10. when we take our eyes off of Jesus

9. UNCOVERING THE SPIRIT OF MAMMON

1. to trust money instead of God
2. Trust
3. financial blessings
4. We succumb to the spirit of mammon by default.
5. True
6. as a resource and a tool for our future
7. True
8. selfish; generous
9. to steal our trust in God
10. paths

10. THE GIVING-TRUST CONNECTION

1. It shows we trust Him.
2. True
3. favor
4. God's blessing never has sorrow attached to it.
5. abundance
6. generosity
7. True
8. He doesn't take into consideration what he has before giving.
9. Giving reflects the nature and character of Jesus.
10. by hearing the Word of God about giving preached over and over again

11. YOUR GIVING IS AN EXPRESSION OF YOUR TRUST

1. True
2. because it is a privilege and a responsibility for those who have received the gift of eternal life
3. because of our love and sense of thanksgiving for what Jesus did
4. from a cheerful heart
5. to the poor and to ministries that help those in need
6. False
7. that we trust Him
8. True
9. because he had great possessions
10. faith in what God says about finances and demonstrating your trust in Him through giving

12. MAKE GOD YOUR TRUST

1. Money
2. that we need to trust Him with our finances
3. god
4. to completely rely on Him
5. to put our trust in money
6. your willingness to give it away
7. because she gave all she had, which indicated she trusted God
8. achieving things in your own ability without God
9. get you to trust in money
10. We all have the same access to the blessings of God, regardless of how long we've been saved, through the blood of Jesus, and we do not reap a curse when we miss the mark.

13. THE MONEY-TRUST CONNECTION: GOD VS. MAMMON

1. money matters
2. by proving to be faithful with finances
3. least; much
4. the importance of faithfulness with money
5. True
6. True
7. because he was more invested in his material possessions than he was the things of God, and was controlled by the spirit of mammon
8. True
9. that your trust is in God alone
10. by purposing in our hearts to give liberally and regularly

14. GIVING: A NATURAL RESPONSE TO GOD

1. natural reflex
2. because it demonstrates trust for God and also activates the spiritual principles needed for your increase
3. giving too little and expecting too much
4. joyfully and abundantly
5. our trust in God; it's a reflection of our awareness of God's grace in our lives
6. stingy
7. giving in proportion to what you've been blessed with by God
8. in percentage and our attitude in giving
9. True
10. True

15. PRINCIPLES OF GIVING
1. True
2. giver; receiver
3. bread and seed
4. It causes them to thank God.
5. helping others
6. True
7. to give it value
8. deciding in advance to give and setting aside the money to do so for a specific purpose
9. True
10. True

16. GIVING: A CHRISTIAN PRIORITY
1. because he was the apostle of grace
2. financial
3. True
4. Tradition
5. False
6. Does it line up with what Paul preached?
7. True
8. our giving
9. Jesus was testing his heart to see if he trusted God.
10. to have resources to give to others

17. THE GIVING PERSPECTIVE

1. True
2. because we recognize what Jesus did for us
3. False
4. a joyful, cheerful attitude
5. Grace
6. because it backs up what we say we believe with action
7. to see their level of trust in God
8. True
9. necessity
10. False
11. because he had been delivered from selfishness and self-effort

18. PARTNERING WITH GOD THROUGH GIVING

1. God's unmerited favor working in our lives
2. seeking what we can give to someone else rather than seeking riches for ourselves
3. They were totally focused on what they could do to help the poor.
4. by giving out of love and thanksgiving rather than out of fear and necessity
5. because they had experienced God's favor
6. The soul becomes enriched.
7. True
8. grace
9. False
10. Gratitude

19. FREE FROM THE SPIRIT OF MAMMON
1. False
2. trusting and focusing on God
3. the spirit of the world that opposes God
4. only trust in God, not money, and rejoice no matter what the circumstances are
5. True
6. to be thankful for what we have, with no thought of what we do not have
7. selfishness
8. contentment; godly lifestyle
9. True
10. False

20. HOW TO BE FREE FROM MAMMON
1. trust it instead of God
2. an evil spirit that wants us to trust money instead of God
3. money becomes destructive
4. to experience higher levels of God's power in our lives
5. least
6. the pursuit of money is your first priority
7. whatever spirit that influences you
8. False
9. trusting in God and His Word
10. when there appears to be lack in your life

21. FREEDOM FROM MAMMON

1. to lure us away from trusting in God
2. lie, cheat, steal, and compromise their values
3. False
4. godly purposes
5. money
6. Trust in God and acknowledge Him in everything; refuse to be wise in our own eyes; honor the Lord with our substance; find wisdom; don't withhold good when it is in our power to do so.
7. pride; poverty
8. True
9. obey God
10. We don't have the grace to deal with the issues of life.

22. CHOOSE GOD OR MAMMON

1. It is negative.
2. True
3. Confusion and instability are the result.
4. debt
5. greater things in the kingdom of God
6. True
7. discontent
8. will of God
9. restoration, supernatural progress, supernatural favor, and a change of status

23. GODLY INFLUENCE ON MONEY

1. trust in Him
2. We open the door to Satan's influence.
3. True
4. loyalty
5. True
6. honor God with your money
7. to assign a heavy weight to it
8. capital or money
9. trusting in God precedes the manifestation of supernatural provision
10. the anointing of God shows up

24. THE PULL OF MAMMON

1. thinking; living
2. True
3. True
4. the influence of the spirit of the world in our financial dealings
5. earth
6. isolate
7. the Word of God
8. False
9. the fear of lack
10. gain; loss

25. CONQUERING THE SPIRIT OF MAMMON: A FIVE-STEP PROCESS

1. reminding ourselves who we are in Christ when the devil tries to tell us otherwise
2. Remember who you are in Christ; locate where your treasure is; decide who you're going to serve—God or mammon; refuse to worry; seek God's kingdom first.
3. True
4. where we are in our walk with Christ
5. True
6. lack; loss
7. heaven; earth
8. Darkness infiltrates your life.
9. True
10. to put His way of doing things first; to honor Him in everything